MAIN MAP

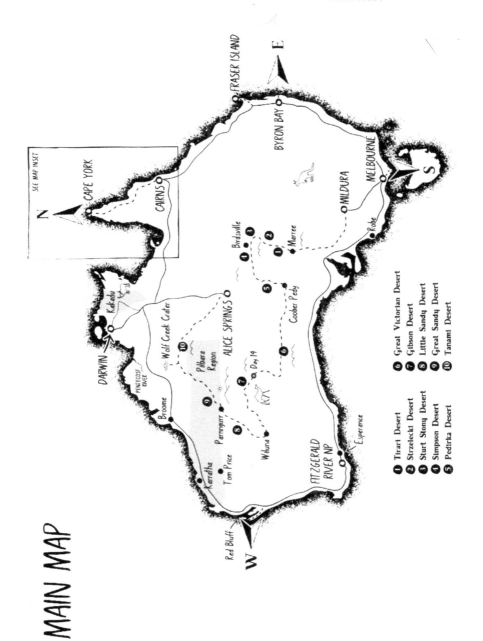

HUNTING FEAR

The adventure of a lifetime

Benji Brundin

This is a work of non-fiction. Names, characters and some places have been changed in order to protect identities.

First paperback edition April 2020
Published by Daring2venture Publications

Book typesetting: Jeremy Strong, Shevek Creative
Map and cover design: David Alenson, Alenson Design
Editing: Liliane Grace, Grace Productions

ISBN 978-0-6487958-0-3 (paperback)
ISBN 978-0-6487958-1-0 (ebook)

www.daring2venture.com.au

This book is dedicated to my mother,
for it was she who gave me the gift of writing and the burning
desire to win.

Be the lighthouse and shine,

and the ships will come to you.

- Unknown

CONTENTS

FOREWORD

Dearest Reader,

My name is Benji Brundin and I am a tradie from Melbourne, Victoria.

I spent the first 33 years of my life just going through the motions, unhappy with what life was serving up to me but also not doing much to change it. I always knew I had drive and ambition yet I sat on the sidelines, waiting for something to happen. I let society and other people tell me what was best for me and how I should live my life. I was a pushover. I didn't have firm opinions on the simplest things, like which music I preferred or even what clothes to wear. I was just another puppet on a string, a cog in the mighty machine, a mindless drone.

Then, a few years ago, I lost everything: love, the graces of society, and the safety of my home. I found myself on the dark side of the alley. To put myself back together I went on a journey across Australia that changed my life. That journey pushed me further than I could ever have known possible, both physically and emotionally. I experienced crippling fear in the face of the unknown, and redemption on the floodplains of Kakadu. What I learnt along the way was so profound that I felt compelled to share it with others.

Thanks for picking up my book. Your curiosity got you this far; I hope my story about what it takes to live life with the throttle wide open keeps you turning the pages. And, just so you know, this book has nothing to do with motorbikes.

Life is a daring adventure.

Cheers,

Benji

HUNTING FEAR

Chapter 1
THE FALL

Good timber does not grow with ease.
The stronger the wind, the stronger the trees.
- Thomas S. Monson

Thursday 10 December 2015

The grass was crisp and cool beneath my bare feet, and I could still smell the fresh clippings as I walked toward our veggie patch in the warm afternoon sun. It was starting to look impressive: the zucchinis seemed to grow bigger every hour and the tomatoes were ripe and juicy – ready to explode. I sat at the edge of my pride and joy, scrunching the grass between my toes, grass I had so lovingly nurtured and watched grow, yet I felt numb to the joy this garden had granted me only weeks, if not days, before.

It was early December 2015, and I had just been stood down from my job in the Victorian Police Academy. With only days left before being sworn in as a constable of police, I'd been cut loose, a 'liability to the upstanding reputation of the Victorian Police'. Now

I sat, rejected, lost, full of loathing and self-pity. *You should never have shown them the book, Brundin!*

I was a failure! What kind of life could I give to my beautiful wife and the family we had talked about having? How could I ever face our friends and family again? The shame!

I'd put so much into being a good squad leader, I'd taken such pride in helping my fellow squaddies when they needed it and had become so close with all of them. Now they'd been ordered not to make contact with me, not to return my calls. I had let everyone down. How could I face my wife? What could I offer her? She would be better off without me.

The garden was in full bloom around me, but I was a mess.

From where I sat, I could see the heads of at least two big batten screws clamping down on the legs of the satellite dish I'd secured firmly to the roof of the house. In the shed I'd built hung a thick industrial power lead and a ladder – all the tools I'd need to get the job done… I shut my eyes and squeezed them hard, trying to get this idea from my tortured mind. And simultaneously I cursed myself for not having the balls to go through with it. Tears crept from the corners of my welded eyelids and my body shook with fear.

Just then the garage door inched open and Scarlett's car drove in. I took a deep breath and did the best I could to compose myself.

"Hey, Babe, how was your day?"

I didn't get up to greet her; I didn't trust my legs to hold me. Instead, I sat on the edge of our garden and tried my best to smile through bloodshot eyes.

As she walked over to me, I could see the pain in her eyes. I could see the worry she felt, and the exhaustion on her face. I was the cause of all of this. I'd kept her awake while I tossed and turned through the nights. Her pain was my fault. She didn't deserve this. I burst into tears and buried my face into my hands. I couldn't look at her.

Scarlett sat on my lap and held me tight. There we sat, husband and wife, sharing grief.

Friday 4th December 2015 – Journal

Ten weeks in the blink of an eye.

I started at the academy with another 22 recruits, all as nervous and scared as each other. During the time we spent together I made some really great mates. We rode the highs and lows together. They even nominated me as a Squad Leader in Week Three! I felt honored that they saw those leadership qualities in me.

I thrived within the academy walls: I clocked the best time in all our fitness tests, I got mid 80s in my first couple of exams and a perfect 100% in the final three, my squad mates liked and respected me.

I told Ms. Leigh, my squad manager, about the memoir I'd written and she was impressed that I had come so far. "Maybe they'll make you a poster boy for Vic Pol – proof that we are bridging the gap between community groups!" were her words. I could even feel my posture starting to change as I walked down the halls of the Academy.

Recruits from other squads started to attend my boxing class on a Wednesday night until I seemed to know everyone. It was all going so well. I aced Gun Week – I was the best shot in the class.

Us recruits went out drinking together and had great times, like wakeboarding with some of the lads on Lake Eildon in Judd's boat. I could feel myself making some great new mates.

I came home every night exhausted after the long days of study, but with a smile from ear to ear. When we had our individual progress meetings with our squad manager I said, "I'm having the time of my life! I feel like I'm really growing into my potential in this place!"

"We can see that, Ben, and that's why I feel the squad are all getting along so well: they see your leadership and enthusiasm, and it filters down through the squad."

Things couldn't have been going any better in life. Scarlett and I had even started trying for a baby.

We had a week of leave and then just one more week and we would be sworn in as constables of police – just before Christmas. We even had our training stations allocated and were getting ready to go into them.

Then, at the last minute, I was called into a meeting yesterday with Inspector B and Senior Sergeant M. M spoke with me on the phone in the morning and told me we were to have a chat about my upcoming book. He sounded warm and friendly on the phone.

Thursday 3rd December 2015, 1500 hours

I am waiting in a boardroom at the academy for M and B. They enter and shake my hand when I greet them.

B: "Hi Ben, how are you? Is this your book?" B holds up a printed PDF copy.

Me: "Yes."

B: "And this is a true account of your life?"

Me: "Yeah."

B: "Okay then. And nothing has been dramatized to make the book more appealing to the reader, or anything like that?"

Me: "No, it's all just how I remember it."

They both scribble furiously on their pads and don't look up at me. I suddenly feel uncomfortable.

Me: "Am I in trouble? I've been as honest as possible..."

M: "We'll get to that shortly."

B: "Ben, your book makes some pretty confronting admissions of illegal activity. How do you think the organization is going to respond to that? There are instances of an assault during a football game, and I quote: 'I cracked him square in the face', and an admission of wrestling your 16-year-old brother... You were twenty-three at the time – that's child abuse. If any of these admissions had been known about during the application process you would never have got in."

Me: "What? No! It was all so long ago and those quotes are out of context!"

B: "'I punched him in the face.' Ben, this is an admission of a serious assault. An indictable offence! If this ever got out, a prosecutor would tear you to shreds in the witness box."

Me: "That happened during a football game when I was

nineteen – and that guy punched me first!"

M: "Did it ever occur to you to mention any of this throughout the process?"

Me: "What? No... I brought a copy of that book into every interview over the two-year process and used it as an example of setting goals and sticking to them. But no one ever asked to read it. It's not like it sounds! The way you're quoting it is all out of context!"

B: "Ben, I read the first few hundred pages of the book, and I can just imagine how hard it must have been growing up in that environment. I applaud your courage. You should be applauded for your resilience and how far you've come. But I have to stand you down. There are admissions of assault and abuse, and family violence is such a huge issue in the media at the moment. Do you think an upstanding citizen acts in this way? The organization will never recruit someone with this sort of past. How do you think you would react if you walked into a house that reflected your own childhood?

"You will be stood down with pay pending an investigation into your suitability as a candidate to hold the office of Constable."

Me: "What? No! I've worked so hard to get here! I'm a good person. I've been a model recruit! You can't do this to me – this is my life you're talking about. I have talked about my past experiences throughout the whole process! Vic Pol could have had this conversation with me over a year ago."

It had taken me nearly six years to write and edit my

first book and I was close to having it published. So many crazy things had happened to me in my early life that I'd become convinced that writing was the way forward for me. I saw myself publishing books and standing in front of rooms full of people, inspiring them to fight for a better life for themselves. I was so clear on this. I knew in my heart that this was what I was supposed to do with my life.

I buried my face in my hands and sank to my knees on the floor as they continued to talk.

B: "Ben, we have pages of references all commending your character, even from high-ranking ex-members. No one is questioning your integrity or your work ethic. But these matters will now have to be investigated."

M: "Ben, as the Inspector said, you should be applauded for your resilience in getting yourself away from that environment. But the admissions have been made now."

Me: "I won't publish the book – I'll burn it! This career means more to me than that book! I want to help people. Can we just make it all go away?"

M: "Ben, do you see what you're asking us to do there? You're asking us to jeopardize our own integrity. Now come on, Benji, get up off the floor. Can you see how we can't do that, regardless of whether the book is published or not? The admissions have been made and we have to take account all of this information."

Me: "I can't believe this is happening. What can I do to get back in the Academy?"

B: "At this point there is nothing you can do. You can

make an appeal to the VPA but in the meantime you will be stood down until further notice."

Me: "For how long?"

B: "At this time of year it will be months."

Me: "What am I going to do now? Where can I work? This is what I'm supposed to do with my life!"

B: "I don't know. Maybe Customs — there are many other options out there. But I highly doubt your case will be successful given the gravity of your admissions, even taking into account your references and results."

Me: "I can't believe this is happening." I slumped on the floor in shock.

B: "As we said, we applaud you. This is nothing personal. We both think you've done an incredible job, but we are just two individuals representing the organization, its values and its best interests."

I spent the next 15 to 20 minutes kneeling in a heap on the floor or standing at the window. I just couldn't believe it. It was over. I felt numb with shock. I called Scarlett and she was stunned. A welfare officer came to check on me and sent me to clean out my locker. As I was getting into my car to make my final departure from this place that was supposed to launch my new shining career, the welfare officer returned and asked me to hand over my ID and lanyard. One final nail in the coffin.

Received a text from Ms. Leigh on the way home:

Hi Ben, I got your message and have just spoken with S/SSgt M. I am sorry. I know how devastated you will be. I unfortunately cannot have a dialogue about this with you now that it has gone to this level and I am involved to an extent. I know you will struggle to understand the reasoning behind the action taken at this time. Know that I think you have had an extraordinarily difficult life and done amazing things that have brought you to a place where you have a wonderful wife and future. There is nothing I can do to help you due to my involvement and actions I have had to take. Please look after yourself and Scarlett. I am thinking of you. Kind regards, Rachel.

So much for being a poster boy for Vic Pol... Instead of being an asset, a model for what was possible, I was to be chewed up and spat out by their risk-averse, politically correct organisation.

December was a pretty tough month for me. I kept running the same tape over and over again in my head: "Life is shit. Nothing works out no matter how hard I try. I'm a failure. You'd be better off without me." I kept repeating this to Scarlett over and over again, and she kept reassuring me that it was not the case. So, then I'd say: "I don't know what you see in me. You can do better than me!" I put Scarlett, and all the people who loved me through hell.

This wasn't the first time she had had to hold me up. My first anxiety attack came in 2012. It was in the peak of the recession and the building trade was in a slump. My first business, in roof tiling, went under. The fact that I couldn't provide a life for my new partner Scarlett, or employ my staff, triggered all my childhood memories of poverty and stealing food. Real fear gripped me. I didn't sleep for a week and spent some time in Emergency at the hospital. Scarlett stood by me the whole time.

Business was too volatile, I decided. The safety and security of the government was the path for me: I applied for the Fire Brigade.

My second attack came just weeks before our wedding a few years later when I received the news that I hadn't been accepted into the Fire Brigade. Once again, the thought of not being able to provide a life for my soon-to-be-wife and one-day-children, set off huge triggers for me.

And now, when we were actually planning to have children, I'd been dismissed from the Police Force. The same triggers from my past were firing off again – in overdrive. I'd thought I finally had it all planned out: secure job, career progression, and hopefully start trying for kids just like all of our other friends. It seemed that my fear of failure was becoming a self-fulfilling prophecy.

Both my parents had struggled with money when I was growing up. My dad had been a homeless bum sleeping in the back of his station wagon. My mum had been a single mother of three working two jobs to make ends meet. She was never home, and I remember there never being any food in the house. We grew up poor, so poor that I would eat the salt and drops of soy sauce when I was hungry. I never wanted to live like that again.

But this was about more than money or a job; I had been seeking family my whole life, ever since I was a kid and left my home for a safer place. For me, the police represented something bigger, something I could be proud of, a place to belong where my morals and virtues would be put to good use. Protect the weak and all of that. I'd always felt a bit lost in normal society, like I didn't really belong. Having come from a shitty household as a kid, I had been searching for that place of belonging my whole life.

My mum had a series of boyfriends after she kicked Dad out. I didn't like any of them. When I was eleven years old Mum and one of her boyfriend's bought a zoo. So we moved our life from the sun-drenched deserts of the Pilbara to the green forests of the Dandenong Ranges. It wasn't as much fun to own a zoo as you might think – lots of work involved! – but I made friends with Jarrod, the son of the couple who lived next door. I was always hanging out at their place and staying for dinner. By the time I was sixteen my mum had moved in with yet another boyfriend and I just wasn't prepared to live with the new guy, so I moved into the saddle shed on Vic and Jen's property and spent the rest of my teenage years living with Jarrod and his family and finishing a roof tiling apprenticeship.

At nineteen, I decided to drive my beat-up old XA Falcon around Australia and go on the adventure of a lifetime. I had it all planned out in my mind: work in the mines in the north-west and on fishing boats in the top end, pick fruit on the east coast and then join the navy. But I never got to chase the adventure-filled life of a navy diver because my mother died suddenly of cancer, so I went back home to raise my 12-year-old brother, Noy.

Vic and Jenny were the people who held my head above water. They took Noy and me in and helped us get on our feet. Vic and Jen have always been the rock I have desperately clung to in the turbulent waters of my life.

I did join the Navy as a reservist when I was 23, a short-lived taste of service life that left me craving for more. I was inspired by the elite dive teams that blew stuff up and went ripping through the waves in speedboats, but the reserves paraded a long way from where I lived and seemed to just be a social gathering for old retired dudes who liked to share war stories. That didn't turn me on, and as my new roofing business was going gangbusters, I had to stay focused.

So when I met Scarlett at 25, I'd put the Navy out of my mind. And yet I couldn't seem to give up the desire to work in the services or to find that brotherhood. I continued to apply for emergency service jobs (the Fire Brigade, the Army Reserves, the Defence Forces, the Airport Fire Services…) and was constantly putting my life on hold while I went through application process after application process.

But despite testing well over that six-year period, something always seemed to lock me out. Often it was red tape or frustrating rules. The Fire Brigade stated that the reason for my unsuitability was the fact that I had received six speeding fines over a six-year period. They were all for driving less than 10 km over the limit but the recurrences proved that I 'hadn't learnt my lesson'; in order for me to reapply, I needed to keep a clean record for 12 months. The next week I lost six more points, all for minor offences. I should have called it quits there and then. The universe was telling me loud and clear that the emergency services were not the path for me. But instead, I persevered with the country fire brigade for another three years, and then, in a last-ditch effort, I spent another two years applying to join the Police Force. *They'll take anyone!* I thought.

When they did accept me into their training program, I felt like my dream life was finally coming together. I'd started to make lasting bonds with the men and women I'd met in the Academy; the brotherhood I'd always craved had finally begun to materialise. To have this taken from me so suddenly felt brutal.

January was just as bad as December. My poor wife grew exhausted from trying to keep my spirits up and encourage me to believe that there was something else out there for me. I just couldn't believe it or get myself together.

I hadn't spoken to Vic and Jenny much about my banishment from the Police Force. They'd been concerned about the book I was writing, and I felt ashamed that I hadn't listened to them.

I couldn't even turn to my squad mates. I remember calling one of the guys one day while I was at a low point and just trying to make sense of it all.

"Benny, mate, I can hear the pain in your voice," he said, "but we've been ordered to not make contact with you while you're under investigation. They haven't told us nothing. I'm sorry, mate, we can have a beer when it's all over, but I just got to go."

I had been their squad leader. I had helped tutor them in the early mornings. I'd led the march every morning on parade. Now, I was dead to them.

I had sought the brotherhood of men my whole life. I had measured my success as a man by the team and family I was about to grow around me. Now it felt as if all I had desired was lost; it had been taken from me.

In March I met up with an old mate whose business was experiencing astronomical growth. I offered to help him out in the office while I was under investigation, and spent a few weeks writing reports for him. I enjoyed volunteering there as it allowed me to use skills I'd forgotten I had, made me feel needed, and kept my mind off the negative stuff. His positive feedback and offer of a job in the near future helped me begin to feel more hopeful and optimistic.

I had started speaking with my therapist again as soon as I was stood down from the cops. We'd had a long history together, so she knew me well. She was troubled that it had never occurred to her that my book could get me into such a mess.

I could hardly blame her for that – I had been totally upfront and honest about my book throughout the whole two-year application process. I'd even brought a copy to my Psych interview and I'd used it as an example of goal setting in my final interview, and was actually praised for doing so! No one had said anything negative until that very last day, so who could have guessed it was going to be a problem?

"Well, let's look at what is good in your life," she said. "Tell me about your amazing wife."

Scarlett had come with me to this session. I had told Ana so much about her and how she was such a rock in my life, and now I wanted Ana to meet her.

"Life has delivered you a cruel blow, Benji, there is no doubt about that. But look how much love there is here. Look at your beautiful wife and how lucky you both are to have found one another. There is something very special here. Hold onto this, cherish this, and everything else will work out – you'll see."

I looked over to my wife, squeezed her hand and smiled fondly. I definitely had a sense of belonging with Scarlett: she was my soul mate. Scarlett smiled back at me. The months had been hard on her; the lines around her eyes gave her worry away. But I knew Ana was right. We did have that special kind of love; our friends called us a 'power couple'. As long as we had each other, as long as I had Scarlett, I knew we could get through anything.

Scarlet and Benji: 20 October 2008 - 29 March 2016

04 May 2016

Dear Scarlett,

I've finished packing all of my stuff away. In the end I decided to just heap all of my clothes etc. into the wardrobe in the garage. All my trinkets and bits and pieces are in the shed also. That way, if I ever need anything, I don't have to come into the house.

The only thing left inside is filing cabinet stuff; we can worry about that in June.

It's been a hard morning. I am crying again… I vacuumed the floor and cleaned up the dog poo again. I know you hate those jobs and I feel that I am going to miss them.

I've been wandering through the house for most of the morning just looking at everything. Bruce is quite relaxed on the deck; he hasn't looked so content this whole past month.

I also tidied up the timber for the deck so there's a bit more room to move down there, and I got the putty for the plaster out of the shed for your dad. Please ask him to either cut back or remove the vine creeper plants as they will take over the whole fence. I grabbed the hedger out for him and put the brush cutter fuel out so he can find it.

I tried to call him. I know he can't answer and help me. I shouldn't have called. Please tell your parents how grateful I am for all they have done for me. Your dad especially has been a real support at times when I've been down. I love them.

Thank you for being so incredible in my life. They say the person you leave is not the person you marry. That isn't the case in our situation. I fell in love with you because you were the most gentle, kind and caring person I had ever met. You nurtured my rough edges and helped me develop as a person. Even in this low moment when you are going through your own grief, you have been there to support me in mine.

It must have been torture to watch me cry like I did last night. I'm sorry I put you through that. But I welcome the tears; I know they are part of the grieving process. And I have lost the most precious thing in my life.

I find myself crying again. I stop what I'm doing and let the tears come. I take deep breaths and feel them falling off my cheeks. The moment passes, and I finish packing my box and tell myself, Life goes on, Benji. Life goes on.

Thank you for everything, Scarlett.

Love

Benji.

My marriage ended abruptly, like the thud of a guillotine's blade. I didn't see it coming – no one did. One minute I was buying timber to extend our deck, the next minute I was selling the wood on eBay. When I look back now, I can see the red flags in our relationship. But as with my dismissal from the police, I simply wasn't ready for the end. I didn't take it very well at all. I say that without blame; Scarlett also took it badly. We sat together and mourned our marriage on numerous occasions, but for her, it had been on the way out for a while.

Scarlett comes from a long line of artists, teachers, musicians and performers, all highly educated and academic. She loves the arts and theatre and has a really gentle, nurturing side to her personality. At her family gatherings we would talk about music and politics, and have deep intellectual discussions about feminism, equality, immigration and other world issues. I'd smile and wing my way through the maze of big words and bold statements, and somehow hold my own.

As for me, well, I was the middle child of a single immigrant mother and a Swedish father who'd been a truck driver in the mines. He'd also been an alcoholic social misfit who was 'on the spectrum'. I was a high school dropout, a boxer, and a roof tiler. I used to steal food so my siblings and I could eat. I came to the relationship with a whole bag of unresolved childhood issues. Regardless of how you framed it, I had always been that guy from the other side of the tracks in our relationship.

We were different. We liked different things: I always wanted to get outdoors and climb the biggest mountains; Scarlett never came camping with me. When we did travel, I'd be up early looking at maps, saying, 'Let's go here and let's go there!' She would sleep in and want room service. She had supported me in my desire to join the Police, although she'd actually hated the idea of me being a cop. She knew me, and knew I would throw myself into the job like a bull at a gate, and that had scared her. As we grew into ourselves, it was just natural that we would grow apart. One of the things she said that stuck with me was: "Benji, I hold you back. One day, when all of this is over, you will see that."

I was still far from seeing it when I moved back up into the hills, back to Jarrod's house and into his spare bedroom. I remember feeling like I'd gone back 15 years in time. The same people still worked at the local supermarket. It was just a small country town but I felt so ashamed. I couldn't walk down the street and look people in the eye. I'd lost my job, my home was gone, and my wife had left me... I was 33 years old and felt like a total failure. It was horrible. At night, in the cold dark of Melbourne's winter, I would light a small fire down by the shed and stare into the flames by myself for hours, numb with the pain of all that loss.

I can still remember having a drink at the local football club one Saturday night. I had played over 100 games there so I still knew most of the people around the place. I felt such shame that it took all of my courage to go in. I was having a drink with someone when one of the older guys stumbled over to me. I could tell he'd been drinking since lunchtime. It was as if, in the ten years I'd been gone, he had never left the place. He still wore the same clothes and had the same smirk on his face as he walked up to me, looking for a bit of fun.

"Benny Brundin! Mr Memoir. I hear you're writing books these days. How's that working out for you?" The old vet waited for me to take the bait, but I refused to acknowledge his remark. To his credit, the guy I was talking with continued our chat as if he hadn't heard the local, who giggled at his own joke and staggered away through the crowds. I ignored the comment and showed no emotion on my face, but my blood was boiling. I didn't stay long after that.

I'd left that town nearly ten years earlier feeling that I was destined for bigger and better things. Where others saw their futures playing out in the small community hub, I had always wanted something different, like being a Special Forces soldier, or working in far-off places saving lives – something more than being just another cog in the machine. But here I was, still a cog.

In June, I decided to go and spend some time in the Philippines. Years earlier I had taken my mother's ashes home, and now I felt that I wanted to be close to her. After over 24 hours in transit, I finally walked into her home village deep in the Visayas region of the Philippines. The old people greeted me with tears in their eyes. They grabbed my face and squeezed my cheeks. For them, I was a window into their sister. I had her eyes, her smile. They could sit with her while they spoke with me. I brought enough food to feed the village, and as we feasted, the kids hid in the corners, giggling at the foreigner's strange accent.

One day I hiked to the top of the biggest hill in the area, a place called Holy Hill because it had a huge metal crucifix on the top. I sat on that hill and just prayed and prayed to my mum to show me the answers, to show me a sign. I had nothing left in me; I didn't know what I was supposed to do with my life. I was crying every day at that point in my life.

In August, when I was back in Melbourne, the job for my friend whose business was booming didn't work out and I found myself unemployed again. I went to the bank the day I quit and got the biggest personal loan they would lend me based on my last two payslips. I had no intention of ever paying that money back. I just wanted to sink into oblivion and forget my whole shitty existence.

In the mornings I'd wake up dreading the thought of yet another day. I'd always been a pretty motivated kind of guy but now I couldn't even keep on top of my laundry. Before meeting Scarlett, I had owned my own business and employed up to eight men. Now I didn't even know the passwords to my own bank accounts, my Facebook account – she had always taken care of that sort of stuff.

Despite our separation, Scarlett tried her best to help me get back on my feet but that just made it worse for me. Her help made me love her more, which just made me even sadder that I'd lost her.

In November, my dad, who lived in Sweden, passed away suddenly of a heart attack. My cousin called me to tell me the news. It came as no shock to me because he had never taken good care of himself. I had kind of been expecting that call ever since I was a kid. A few days later I was on a plane to Sweden to help arrange his funeral.

My dad was a nice guy. He was a total loser and an alcoholic, but he didn't have a nasty bone in his body. He had lived a very modest, uninspiring life, and had lived alone ever since my mother kicked him out thirty-odd years earlier. He often talked about all the things he was 'gunna' do if he ever won the lottery. He left this world with no real material possessions, and no loving family members standing around his bed.

At his funeral I vowed to myself that I would never live a life like he had. I did not want to end up like him; I wanted to be more than he had ever been. I placed my hand on his coffin and swore to myself that I would live an inspiring and adventurous life – I would fill my life with love and wonder and teach my children how to be the best they could be.

In January 2017 I found myself back in Melbourne. I moved in with my mate Whitey for six to eight weeks while I sorted out the last of my separation. Whitey was awesome – he was such a good mate to have around at the time. We were both sure that it was only going to be a matter of weeks before my divorce was finally sorted, and I could move on with my life. I had tried desperately to win Scarlett back, but it was clear that our marriage was well and truly over. The solicitors were getting into everything now, like vultures over the dead carcass of our shared life. That hurt me; the betrayal in that cut deep.

I was roofing again and I hated my job. I'd lost everything that inspired me. There was just nothing for me to love anymore. All I wanted to do was run away and escape the bullshit reality I was faced with. I spoke with Victor, the man who had been a father figure to me for most of my adult life. He had a way of making things happen or knowing the people who had the answers.

"Vic, I want to buy a van and just get out of here. Do you know anyone who has one for sale?"

"I'll keep an eye out," he told me.

The next day he found a van for me; the day after that I borrowed some money from him and Jenny, and bought it.

The van was a 2003 Ford Transit, long wheelbase, mid-roof turbo diesel. A courier's truck, it had belonged to one of Vic's mates since it was new. I picked it up at a bargain price because it had an issue with the accelerator that no one had ever been able to fix – no mechanic, not even the dealership. Vic found the problem and fixed it with a cable tie in about ten seconds.

The van was a blank canvas, and I started to kit the interior out with a bed and a fridge and power every chance I got. Now that I was roofing again, I was always on building sites so the whole van was pieced together with leftover building material, especially recycled timber. Hundreds of roofing screws held it together. *This is the vessel that is going to take me away from all of this, and project me into my new existence!* I told myself.

I started going away in that van as often as I could. I would park in a campground somewhere and start cutting bits of timber and screwing them together. People must have walked past and wondered with mild amusement why someone would come all the way out to the middle of the bush just to bang away with drills and handsaws.

But it wasn't all fun and focus. I remember sitting in the back one morning in a car park by the beach. Outside, I could hear people chatting and laughing together as they strolled down to the foreshore. Inside my van I sat on the ribs of the floor and cried uncontrollably. I was completely alone.

Throughout the first half of that year, the solicitors' letters started to fly back and forth. Ask anyone who has ever been through a divorce and they will tell you it's not pretty. In the wake of my career crisis and my father's funeral, it was a lot to absorb. Sometimes I would call Jenny. "Jenny, I'm done. I just don't feel like I belong anywhere," I'd sob into the phone. She would listen and keep telling me that I had people who loved me everywhere, but I was too distraught to hear her words. She and Victor were incredible during this time in my life. I leaned on them both heavily, and they just kept holding me up and were always there for me.

Around March, another legal fight popped up. I'd had an investment property built six years earlier and it had almost immediately begun to fall apart. The concrete foundations had been poorly poured, causing the whole house to lean to one side. I had been fighting the construction company for years, trying to get them to fix it, and now, after six years of getting the run-around, their solicitors sent me a letter simply denying liability.

So, here is a fun little fact for those of you screaming, 'What about your Builders Insurance!' Your Builders Insurance only covers you if your builder has become insolvent. In that case, you just need to prove the fault, and then you get a cash payout amount. My builder was still operating and building hundreds of homes per year. For a big builder like that, it was simply a numbers game. They knew that the process of taking them to court would be a very long and drawn-out one, costing me, the homeowner, in excess of $30,000.00 and another two to three years of dealing with government agencies and solicitors. For most people, this kind of additional pain and suffering puts the whole issue in the too-hard basket, so they will sell. They will cut their losses and let it become someone else's problem… and the big nasty builder wins.

So, there I was with solicitors coming at me from both sides. I had lost everything – even my dog Bruce had gone to stay with Scarlett because I simply didn't have the lifestyle to support him, and now I had this builder trying to rob me of my life savings too. The worst of it was that I didn't have an ounce of fight left in me. I felt broken, betrayed and lost, and I just couldn't be bothered anymore. I did what any bloke would do: I grabbed a beer and had a few drinks.

The rest of that year seemed to go by in one giant foggy haze. I was reckless and irresponsible, quite often waking up in the back of my van parked out the front of a pub or down some side street, and not knowing how the hell I got there. Shades of my dad…

There was no structure in my life, no discipline, and I suffered because of it. I had once been the only guy in my navy recruiting squad to pass a locker inspection. Now, amidst all the chaos, I had to smell my clothes to see if they were clean or not, and I couldn't even find a pair of socks among all the crap piled up in the corner of my room. I just kept on living as if tomorrow was the day I was going to make a break for it and escape. My eight weeks at Whitey's became fourteen months.

Thank God for the support of Vic, Jenny and my incredible friends. They would listen to me ranting and raving, and just let me vent. I don't know where I'd be now if I hadn't had them in my corner.

Finally, in September, Scarlett and I got rid of the solicitors and sat down together to come to an agreement. We sorted it out with a handshake over the dining room table. I should have been relieved, but it still hurt me to see her.

We sold the house in December and our divorce was finalised on the 31st of that month, nearly 21 months after Scarlett had initiated the separation and almost two years since I'd been dismissed from the Police Force. Those milestones marked the end of a chapter of my life.

I spent most of the months of December and January out of my mind. Looking back, I was a bloody mess.

I knew I was in trouble when I woke up on a park bench one Sunday afternoon, after my best friend's buck's party. I was covered in piss and spew. And it wasn't just any park bench: it was in the car park of a church. It was 2 p.m. and kids and parents were running around after their morning church service. I only woke up because the heat of the midday sun was beating down on me. My nostrils were blocked with the remnants of last night's souvlaki, my shoes splattered with sauce, bile and half-eaten food. And yes, I had actually pissed my pants. I stumbled away from the church people, wondering what the hell they must have thought.

On the tram ride back to Jarrod's house, people moved away from me. I couldn't blame them: I was sweating profusely, my eyes were bloodshot and weeping, I reeked of vomit and piss, and I couldn't stop dry retching. I had to keep getting off the tram to throw up in the nearest gutter. I was shaking from the effort of it all. Around me, women walked past with bags of shopping and designer clothes, and families sat with their dogs as they ate their lunch in the street cafés. They were appalled. And so was I. It was the rock-bottom moment of my life.

From a very early age I had been conditioned to be the protector in my family, the provider, the guardian. Family was very important to me, and I took my role very seriously. I can still remember so clearly when my mum kicked my dad out. I remember the words he said to me as he was packing his car: "Look after your sister and your mother, son; you're the man of the house now." I was five years old.

When I was thirteen, my mum left my brother and me with her boyfriend for a few months while she started a new business in the Philippines. Her words were similar: "Look after your brother, Benji; I'll be back in a few weeks."

And I can still remember the last words I spoke to her when she passed away suddenly: "You give me such strength, Mum. You have such proud sons. I'm a proud man and Noy will grow up to be one. You don't have to worry about him; I promise I will take care of

him. We love you, Mum, and we will always be together. I swear it."
I was nineteen.

Family *was* important to me, but now my little brother was all grown up and the new family I had been about to create was lost to me. In the wake of the police issue, I was a soldier without an army. And now that my divorce was confirmed, I was a shepherd without his flock. Never in my life had I felt so lost.

Jan 31ˢᵗ 9.31 p.m. – Home from Rainbow Serpent Festival

Feeling exhausted.

It has been two weeks of chaos and excessive partying, and as a result I am feeling extremely emotionally fragile. Received emails from Scarlett while I was away that show there is nothing left. There is no reason to contact her, no reason to talk. It is done and over. She was, is, the love of my life, but she is gone from me forever. I need to get my head together. I need to step back from the booze and the partying and let my brain heal. You have the opportunity to do and be whatever you want to be in life and you are making a mess of yourself. Let's start now, Benji.

A week after writing that journal entry I was on another bender, this time at my best mate's wedding. What a joke I was turning out to be. While everyone was getting ready to go home and let the newlyweds be, I was getting loose with a few of the bridesmaids. I ended up going out all night and then beating myself for being such a mess and having no will power to say no. I was beating myself up about that almost daily…

The next weekend I knew I had to get out of town, or no doubt I would be back in the pub, making the same bad decisions. I began to think much more seriously about taking off on that trip around Australia. Poring over a map of Australia, it occurred to me that touching the four compass points of the mainland would be a fun focus for the trip.

The westernmost point was a place called Steep Point, aptly named for the steep cliffs that surrounded the narrow peninsula. It was located hundreds of kilometres from any township, and across endless sand dunes. The northern point, Cape York, was just as wild and isolated, and regarded as one of the last true odysseys in the world. The eastern point was located in a car park in Byron Bay, NSW, so it wasn't going to be an issue to get to that one. Fraser Island, however, was further east along the coast and only separated from the mainland by a few hundred metres of water; I figured that the lighthouse on Fraser Island would be my eastern challenge. And the southernmost point was located in my home state of Victoria at Wilsons Promontory. I'd never been there, so I decided that was a good place to start my trip.

By then the van had been ready and waiting to get out on the open road for quite a few months. It was a nuisance driving something so big around town all the time, so I thought a motorbike would make short trips for the groceries much easier. I'd never really ridden a motorbike, so when I came back to my mate's house one day with a little postie bike, they all laughed out loud.

"What the hell are you going to do with that? You'll bloody kill yourself, mate."

They were being totally honest with me. They knew I had a habit of making impulsive decisions, and this was a perfect example.

The postie bike didn't pass its road worthy test so it ended up on the farm. I was spewing. And then one of the guys from the gym told me about Bike Sales, an online store that listed all types of motorbikes for sale. On the first page I found an adventurous-looking bike with white plastic covers and off-road tyres. It was located only 10 km from my place. I called the seller and arranged to stop in on my way home.

It was a stock standard 2008 Yamaha, WR250R with 5000 km on the clock. At the time, I knew nothing about bikes. I'd thought that Yamaha made guitars. Turns out that the same company makes musical instruments *and* motorbikes. It also turned out that the owner of the bike was selling all his gear as well.

I tried the gear on: two silk shirts, riding pants, two helmets, Alpinestar motocross boots, body armour… it all fit me like a glove. And it came with a spare chain, oil, and a Yamaha racing gear bag.

"Take it for a spin and see what you think."

There I was in full motocross riding kit, having never ridden a 250 before, cutting laps up and down the streets of inner-city Coburg. Perfect illustration of *all the gear, no idea!*

When I turned back into the driveway, feeling good, the guy said: "It also comes with this bike rack that slots into your tow ball hitch."

Sometimes, you have little wins in life; this was one of those times. It was just meant to be.

I bought that bike on the spot. It was the only bike I ever looked at, and at the time of writing, aside from the postie, still the only bike I have ever ridden. Best $3,300.00 I've ever spent. I lovingly named her Whiskey, which translates as 'water of life' in Gaelic. The irony of that would not be lost on me in the deserts 18 months later.

I added a 12-volt cigarette charger for my phone, and I took the cargo rack and pannier bags off my little postie bike and modified the frame to bolt them to the tail of my WR. Those were the only modifications I made to it.

So, after work on that Friday, I loaded my newly registered bike up with a backpack, some camping gear in my postie pannier bags, and some fuel, and set off towards the Prom. That 200 km would be an epic bloody journey for me considering I'd be figuring out how to ride *en route*!

What could possibly go wrong? I thought. Little did I know that this excursion would become the start of my adventure of a lifetime.

Chapter 2
SOUTH POINT, WILSONS PROMONTORY

Fortune favors the bold.

- Virgil

Wilsons Promontory is arguably one of the most beautiful national parks in Australia. Black cockatoos fly through the air against a backdrop of huge granite mountains and thick jungle vegetation. Riding through dense coastal bushland you feel like you're heading into a lost world. Wallabies and kangaroos line the road close enough to touch and unfazed by human presence. This interaction with the local wildlife is something the park is famous for. Despite large numbers of tourist and hikers, the native animals are quite trusting and very little rubbish disturbs their habitat. The park is superbly managed.

When you reach the coastline of white sandy beaches and

rugged headlands, islands litter the horizon on both sides. Friends of mine surf there and quite often remark how calming it is to sit on their boards with dolphins in the surf around them and watch wombats shuffle along the sand. It's a place unlike any other in Victoria.

By the time I reached the little store at Tidal River campgrounds it was shut, which meant I couldn't get any more supplies. I only had five cans of tuna with me. Shit! I thought. Not exactly gourmet nutrition. I hadn't really thought this trip through…

Instead of shopping, I went for a walk down the beach to sit with my thoughts for a while. I sat with my legs crossed and tried to meditate for five minutes. I was hopeless at meditation but I did feel more relaxed every time I tried to zone out, and meditating somehow helped me center my thoughts. I reached out to my mum again and asked her to help show me the way forward. I still felt so lost in the world.

Once I'd finished my beach walk, I planned to park my bike and hike the mountain and the twenty-odd kilometres down to that southernmost point and back again. I hiked to the top of Mount Oberon, which is only 3.5 km each way, but I pushed hard and was sweating (and starving) as I climbed the last few steps to the top. When I summited, as if on cue, the clouds blew over and completely blocked out the view down below. I shrugged my shoulders and took a seat; all I could do was wait. I sat patiently and waited with a few other hikers, and then suddenly a ray of sunlight broke through and lit up the mountaintop. My face immediately felt warm, and in that moment, calmness and peace pervaded as I watched the rest of the clouds drift away and expose the breathtaking view below.

I enjoyed one of the best sunsets in the state that day. *This sure beats getting drunk,* I thought to myself, and ate two of my precious cans.

I left the summit and returned to the car park to grab my tent and supplies. Then I started the hike to South Point. I hiked through the dark to a campsite some 20 km away. Throughout that night I felt real fear. The reality was that I was on a well-maintained gravel track in one of the most visited and busy national parks in Australia, but I felt as if I was alone in the middle of nowhere. It was pitch black and raining a little. A fog settled over the track. Many times I stopped and thought that turning back to the car park would be the safer option; I came up with a million reasons to turn back.

You haven't prepared for this hike, Benji! You're wearing board shorts for Christ's sake! You have no food, not much water, and it's a long way… You might not even be on the right track! You'd better turn around… You shouldn't be out here. You're not a bloody hiker. You can't even do your laundry. You're not cut out for this. Turn around, you idiot! You'll get lost out here!

And then, at some point during that night, another voice came back to me. One I hadn't heard in a long time.

No, Brundin. You can f#@king do this! Keep walking. You read the map right. You've only got three cans of tuna, but you had a big lunch before you left home. You won't die of starvation. It's cold but there's only six hours until the sun comes up. Keep walking and you'll win. If you turn around now, then that's it. You go back to the pub and that's what will become of your life. You can be better than you have been. You can do this. Keep walking, mate, and we can get there together.

That was a tough night. Torn by the demons in my head, I nearly did turn back a few times. My phone had no reception so it was just me, the darkness, and my tormented thoughts. Finally I stumbled on blistered feet into the campground. I pitched my tent and slept like a dead man.

The next morning I made it down to South Point. Standing on the edge of the continent, I yelled into the howling wind: "I'm free! I'm freeeeeeee!" The words were victorious, but my tone lacked conviction.

Nonetheless, I felt like I had turned a corner during the night. Riding my new bike and going on that long first hike felt like quite the achievement, almost an initiation rite.

Although my divorce had been finalised in January, by March I still hadn't left on the trip I'd been going on about for over a year. It became an ongoing joke. Whenever my brothers or Vic and Jenny would see me, they'd ask, "Have you got to Darwin yet?"

I knew I was equipped to go, but I kept making excuses to stay. Even though my life was a mess and I felt I'd become a burden to the people who loved me, turning my back on everything I knew and venturing into the unknown alone was one hard leap to take. I still felt so caught up in shame and embarrassment that I suspected I would never return to Melbourne, and the finality of that thought was why I felt so scared about leaving.

My whole life was packed into my van: birth certificates, passports, everything. When Scarlett and I split, I let her keep all the material stuff; it meant nothing to me without her. I felt no connection to society either. I was done! I had given my all and done everything society had asked of me. I'd worked hard, I'd invested in property, I'd been a loving and faithful husband, and despite all that, I had lost it all. I had followed all of society's rules and ticked all the boxes, and been kicked in the arse.

And yet, on some deep level, I had never felt that that was the life I wanted to live. I was 'happily unhappy'. Scarlett had seen this in me. I'd always wanted her to come on adventures with me and do crazy things, but it just wasn't in her. In a way, wanting a divorce was her only way of pushing me to commit to what I wanted.

I remember the day I finally did get into my van and start out on the road. I had helped a friend with a big working bee at his place. When we'd finished I did the rounds and shook everyone's hand goodbye. They all wished me luck in a non-committal kind of way – they'd heard me going on about this trip for months but I don't think anyone believed I was actually going to go.

I pulled over a dozen times to check and recheck that everything was okay. My stomach was tied up in knots and I had diarrhoea for the first few days on the road. I chewed my nails down to stumps, and I woke up with headaches those first days too. My body was screaming at me to turn back but I knew I couldn't.

Instead, I turned my back on the world and on painful memories. I just wanted to drive my van as far away from all of it as I could.

Van Build: https://www.youtube.com/watch?v=aQCf1B-TyU8

BB – KEY #1: A GOAL

Would you believe that even as a kid I had always wanted to write a book? My mum was a writer and she'd always encouraged me to write. But I kept my passion for writing to myself as I grew because I felt I would be laughed at; writing just wasn't a manly thing to do. Now, does hiding myself away from the world serve me – or anyone else, for that matter? I mean, what would you be reading right now if I hadn't been authentic with myself and announced that I was going to write a book?

So ask yourself: *What would I truly love to do? What is my dream for my life? What is the legacy I would like to leave?*

The truth is, I was never actually destined to be a cop. The universe had kept shutting those police/navy/army/fire brigade doors because they weren't my true calling. Once I stopped trying to force those doors open and instead paid attention to what I *really* wanted to do, everything started to flow.

You need to trust that the universe has your back. Things will flow when you're on track. Open yourself up to the possibility that the only thing holding you back from your dream is you, and ask yourself why. Face up to whatever the fear or concern is. Define your desire as clearly as you can (but don't worry about how you're going to achieve it). Then announce your intention, your goal, to the world!

Once you have announced what it is that you want

to do with your life, you can expect ridicule; you can expect people to try to shut you down. Absolutely! How many people do you think looked at me, the tradie, and scoffed at the idea of *me* writing a book?

But you will also receive encouragement, and people who are aligned with what you want to achieve will start to come into your life. These people will hold you accountable, even if it is in the form of giving you grief about yet another crazy idea. Your shame or pride will make you take action, but if you keep the plan to yourself, who will push you forward? How can the right people come into your life if the world doesn't know what it is you want to achieve?

Step One to success and a new life is to decide what you would truly love to do and announce your intention!

Building my van. Early 2017.

The day I bought my bike December 2017. All the gear, no idea.

Most southerly point of mainland Australia

Sunset from the top of Mount Oberon.

Chapter 3
THE RISE

Feel the fear and do it anyway.

- Susan Jeffers

My van had been through quite the transformation over the past 12 months. I had originally planned to just throw a mattress in the back, plug a fridge in, and take off. But since the divorce took so long to finalise, I had lots of time to build. I built, dismantled and rebuilt it half a dozen times until it resembled something I could be proud of.

From the outside it looked like a tradie's truck with scratched and faded paintwork and a huge 3m x 2m custom roof rack sitting on top. Vic had made the rack for me, and there was not another roof rack like it in the world. It was strong, with mesh welded to the ribs to allow people to walk across the top. I've had up to eight people sitting on top of my van, star-gazing with a few beers, and it never even flexed. It had an access ladder – again custom-built by Vic – hanging from the rear door; a motorbike rack jutting out the back; a 20-inch light bar at the front; LED lights around the whole perimeter of the roof rack; and a floodlight out the back. The floodlights came on when it was in reverse so at night I'd be able to see what was behind me in my reversing camera, and the light bar would make driving across the deserts at night a breeze. Tool boxes for additional storage on top, alongside solar panels for consistent 12-volt charging when the van was parked for extended periods. It had a Fiamma 3.2 metre awning on the side that I'd swapped for a bottle of rum, and the quote, 'Life is either a daring adventure or nothing at all' splashed across the side sliding door.

The walls and ceiling of the interior had been filled with the best quality roofing insulation money could buy, panelled with seven-millimetre plywood and then finished with blue marine carpet. It was warm inside even when the snow was falling on the mountains outside.

I'd made a walnut woodgrain desk and pantry out of leftover wardrobe doors; the same woodgrain provided flooring and drawers that tucked neatly away under the double bed for all my clothing and computer equipment, and I'd installed a polished woodgrain bench that pulled out of the rear doors on a double slider to prepare all my food on.

A wooden shelf that ran the length of the driver's side wall could have told its own story: it was made from wood salvaged from sand dunes on the coastline of Phillip Island, and it weighed a tonne. Surfboard hooks along the other interior wall provided more hanging space. Downlights throughout gave me enough light to work at the desk or read a book in bed and not have to get up to turn the lights off. A huge deep-cycle truck battery powered the fridge, LED lights, and over 10 power points. I installed a 240-volt air-conditioning unit for those hot summer days, and strip lighting along the floor of the shelf. When it was dark, this light would shine out of the knotholes and onto the wine glasses that hung underneath it.

The ceiling had blue LED strip lighting that lit up the perimeter of a huge ancient map of the world that a friend and I had vinyl-wrapped ourselves, and I'd attached a three-metre long vinyl-wrapped picture of El Nido Bay in the Philippines to the passenger wall. The van was windowless so it was good to wake up and look out at that view every morning. On the rear door I hung a street sign I'd 'found' on the side of the road. So now, my new address was Number 1 Gypsy Lane.

At the rear of the van there were two huge sliding drawers that held tools, spare parts, radiator hoses, fan belts, motorbike tubes, kitchen utensils, and all those other bits and pieces you might need one day. It had hooks on the doors that held my helmet, backpacks and utility belts. My riding gear stashed away neatly in its own compartment under the bed, as did the gas cookers and table. A comfortable double futon mattress, and I was set to go.

The van was over six metres long, over three metres high, and weighed over three tonnes. It was now my home. I loved it, and would fuss over it daily with little things that needed adjusting here or replacing there. I knew every screw, cable, nut, nook and cranny in it. It was my baby, my pride and joy.

The day that I finally left Melbourne I followed the coast road west and onto the Great Ocean Road. I stopped there for a few nights to camp with friends but I had seen the GOR dozens of times; it was beautiful, yes, but old news for me. My first stop outside of Victoria was a little town in South Australia called Robe.

A friend of mine back home had told me adamantly: *When you get to Robe, you have to take your bike out onto the beach. You'll love it!*

But then I'd think: *If you take your bike out now and hurt yourself, then forget about your trip, it's over. You'd best wait until you've seen a little more.*

I can still remember chewing what was left of my nails down even further as these voices did battle in my head. Finally this voice won: *No, Brundin! Get your gear on, buddy! This is what we signed up for! You wanted adventure – well, here it is. You don't know how to ride? Well, let's go and find out how!*

At that time, I had only ever ridden in riding boots once. I had cleaned my air filter three times. And yet I got my bike off the van and rode away into the sandy tracks of the Little Dip Conservation Park, white knuckles gripping the bars.

I bumped and banged my way up the tracks, with my legs sticking out either side to help steady the bike. That bike was taking *me* for the ride, that was for sure! I finally got out onto a beach and remembered what Billy had told me: *Ride down near where the water meets the sand; it's firmer there.*

I rode down a track and came out to a particular beach that had quite a steep entry into the water. I made a v-line straight for it, thinking it would be easier going down there. As I approached the edge of the wet sand, my front wheel began to dig in and bog down. I turned the wheel hard and aimed it back towards the top of the beach, revving the engine to get away from the salt water. The back wheel just bit in hard. I was bogged.

I jumped off, and with the water breaking around my boots, started frantically trying to push the bike up the beach. That was hard bloody work! The sand was deep and rutted along the whole beach. I had never ridden off-road, let alone in deep sand; I didn't know how. So I revved the bike in first gear and jogged along next to it in the hope that the sand would eventually firm up. After about 500 metres of this, I was well and truly buggered. Breathing hard and drenched in sweat, I decided to take a break.

I walked down to the water's edge, wet my face and sat on the sand. After a moment I turned and looked back up at my bike. My options were grim: if I turned around, I would be straight back into the deep stuff but it was only a kilometre or so back to the track; on the other hand, if I went straight ahead, the deep sand might go on forever!

I was out in the middle of nowhere. I hadn't seen a car at all that day. I was in deep shit and it was all on me to get out. Despite my exhaustion, there was something exhilarating about this. I laughed out loud. *Brundin! You're in this now! Let's get on with it!*

I kept on pushing my bike forward like a jockey pushing his trusted steed to win. But while that took me off the beach, I found myself on another sandy, rutted bush track. I kept on, fighting the bike through the sand, and finally, eventually, the sand did firm up again.

The secret to riding successfully through sand is that you have to go fast and lean back. I didn't know any of this at the time, nor did I have the confidence to go very fast. So I just did my best to hang on. I can remember cresting the top of yet another dune and seeing a tiger snake baking in the sun right in my path. At the moment I saw it, I was just a passenger on my bike, 'tank slapping'[1] across the track. There was nothing I could do to avoid the snake but luckily it shot off back into the bush.

I arrived at a fork in the track and had a decision to make. I had tried unsuccessfully to ride across two beaches by then. I had pushed my bike up countless sandy hills, my water was almost gone, and my forearms were aching from gripping the bars so hard. I knew that a left turn would most likely take me onto another beach, and a right would take me back to my van and out of this torture.

Let's get it done, Brundin!

That voice in my head convinced me to have just one more go.

This beach started like all the others: soft, rutted sand. Immediately I thought I had made a mistake. But then it hardened, and I was suddenly riding on firm, flat sand at the edge of softly breaking waves.

Ask anyone who has ever ridden on the beach and they will tell you there is something very exhilarating about it: the salt air in your face, the simple naked beauty of riding on the edge of the water, the waves washing up against your front wheel. It's a special feeling. I must have ridden back and forth along that beach a dozen times. *Wooohoooo!* I was suddenly unaware of the exhaustion and pain in my body. I was like a kid on Christmas day. I was hooked.

The beaches and sand dunes of Robe really tested me, and like the hike to South Point, I pushed myself past what I thought I was capable of. With every victory, my destroyed self-worth was returning. That first ride out into the wild places really set the tone

---

1   Tank slapping is when the bike is wobbling beneath the rider and the handlebars oscillate wildly. The rider's knees repeatedly hit the tank on each side.

for the rest of my trip: I decided that, no matter what, I wouldn't turn back, I wouldn't give into my fear!

My journey west took me across the Nullarbor Plain (in South Australia) and onto the beaches of Esperance and LeGrand National Park (Western Australia). And let me tell you, of all the beaches I have since ridden on, Esperance is one of the most visually beautiful coastlines in all of Australia. LeGrand National Park honestly looks like a setting straight out of a Jurassic Park movie.

I rode my bike along over 20 km of beautiful, hard, packed white sand in Le Grand. It was a stunning day. Crystal blue waves were curling beautifully in the offshore breeze. I sat back in my seat and twisted the throttle wide open. I felt magnificent. My heart was healing.

A few days later I was driving into the Fitzgerald River National Park.

The FRNP is situated on the southern coastline of Western Australia. It's approximately 200 km from any town in any direction. It is bloody remote. One of the largest National Parks in the country, it has a diverse landscape of rolling plains, colourful breakaways, rugged peaks and headlands, and stunning beaches and coastline.

The road into the Park was in such poor condition that I could only manage around 20 to 30 km an hour. The ruts were like small mountains. My back doors shook open and filled my van with a thick layer of fine red dust. Eventually I had to admit defeat. I parked on the side of the road at the start of a 4x4 track. And those little voices started again…

Turn around now… or see what's down this track?

Brundin! You've got nothing left to lose! This is what you signed up for, mate! Get the bike off!

Riding down that track was complete insanity. Looking back, I really wasn't in a very stable state of mind. Despite all the people back home who had loved me and supported me through my divorce, I was still so caught up in my own head that I honestly believed I had nothing and no one in the world, and that if I died or disappeared, my absence would simply unburden everyone. I had no beacon, no way of contacting anyone; no one even knew where I was in the world. If things went bad, they would have been very bad for me.

I rode down that track for what felt like forever, bum on the seat and legs kicking the sand up either side of the bike, just praying to stay upright. Eventually the track brought me out onto some stunning cliffs. Huge granite boulders dropped sharply into the water like the gatekeepers of the coast, keeping the rolling swell at bay.

I rode down this steep hill, my back wheel locked the whole way, and into a small clearing. Parked the bike and walked out onto the beach. It was incredible. I was at the end of the world, in an ancient kingdom. The beach was about 200 metres of pure white sand and flanked by colossal rocky cliffs. The water was crystal blue. A huge swell crashed repeatedly into the cliff walls, disintegrating into a million tiny droplets. The noise of the water echoed off the cliff walls like a cauldron of thunder. At the rear of the sandy beach was the mouth of a river, but it was cut off from the surf. When I walked over to check this out, I could see fish as big as my forearm just cruising past, totally unfazed by my presence. I could have scooped them up. It was paradise. I imagined what it would have been like for a sailing ship wrecked and marooned here. Who would ever want to leave? Everything you might need was here. This was a river that the Indigenous Australians would have lived on. I couldn't help smiling to myself.

I stripped naked and ran up and down the beach like a child. I was thirty-four but living wrecklessly had made me soft and overweight. I hadn't shaved in weeks and the bald patch on my skull seemed to grow bigger by the day. For too long I'd felt middle-aged, washed-up, and a burden to society. But now I jumped into the surf, threw my hands into the sky, and roared.

When I was fourteen years old one of my mother's boyfriends poured a mug of steaming coffee all over me, scalding my chest and neck. He had wanted to assert his dominance over me. Without a moment's thought I'd been up on my feet and beating my fists into him over and over again until he was curled up in the foetal position, cowering, his beard bloody, pleading for me to stop. I roared full into his face. "Don't ever come near us again! You have ruined our lives!"

And now here I stood, beating my chest with my fists and roaring that same roar into the surf like a caveman who had just killed his first sabretooth:*"You can't beat me! You can't! I'm still here! I'm still f#@king here! AAAAAARRRRGGHH, AAARRRRGGGHHH, AAAAAAAAAARRRRRGGGGGHHHHH!"* I stood firm like a pillar of stone as the surf crashed over me and washed salty tears from my eyes. I could feel my soul purging the foul rot of self-loathing from its core.

I sat on the beach for an hour or so and let the euphoria of success run its full course. But after a while, I started to feel lonely. Thoughts drifted back to my old life, my garden and Bruce my dog. *He would love it here but she would never have come on this adventure, Benji.*

The image of our house with its picket fence and vegie patch came back to me. I'd always wanted an adventurous life but life had kept me in suburbia, first looking after Noy when Mum died, and then marriage with Scarlett. Sitting there on the dunes, it made sense that I'd felt conflicted as a tomato-grower. I was an adventurer! I'd always wanted adventure, and for whatever reason, I'd deprived myself of it. This time I was going to embrace it! *Your differences are why you're not together. Move on, mate. Own the adventure!*

There was no point staying there any longer. It would have been an amazing place to share with someone, but I just had to accept the fact that I could share it with others by writing about it. And besides, I had other things to worry about, like getting back up the hill.

BB – KEY #2: UNDERSTAND YOUR 'WHY'.

This is very important. Your 'why' needs to be something of substance if it's going to drive you when all seems lost.

Why do you want to achieve whatever it is that you want?

If you want a million dollars and the reason is simply to hoard it all, then chances are you're going to fall short of the mark. But if your reason is because you grew up in poverty and you don't ever want your family to suffer the way you did, then chances are that when the chips are down and you are on Struggle Street, you will somehow find the resources and energy to keep pursuing the path to success.

My 'why' was a deep itch that I felt I needed to scratch: after a childhood of feeling unworthy, I wanted to prove to myself that I *was* worthy.

Without a strong 'why', it is unlikely that you will stick to your goal until completion. So...

Why do you want to achieve whatever it is that you want?

Chapter 4
WEST POINT, STEEP POINT

Struggle is the architect of the soul.

- James Cook

There were certainly times when I felt the loneliness creep in. Sleeping in the bush on my own in the middle of nowhere wasn't so bad; it was the times I was nearest to people that my aloneness really hit home. But for the most part, I found company along the way. For instance, there was Daniel, the young Aussie kid travelling with his dog. He'd felt disconnected and lost, so at the age of 20 he'd bought a ready-made camper and had set off on the road to find himself.

We travelled for three days together through South Australia and the York Peninsula (not to be mistaken for Cape York in Far North Queensland). We sat in the bones of an old shipwreck, drank beers and watched the sun set over a flotilla of small boats at harbour. He told me all about his life and his struggle to find meaning in it.

"Don't worry, mate, you'll work it out," I said. "This trip will help you discover what you want in life, I can assure you."

Who the hell was I to be giving life advice? Ha!

Daniel was really at the mercy of the luck gods. He had been travelling for eight weeks and didn't even know how to check his tyre pressure. I showed him how to check that, and his oil and water. When we parted, I gave him one of my old tow straps and wished him safe travels.

Then there were Jett, Koda and Talon. These young lads were on the trip of a lifetime from Edinburgh University in the UK. We met in a laundromat in Margaret River, Western Australia. They'd just finished university and had decided to travel Australia together. We spent the better part of a week surfing (them trying unsuccessfully to teach me) and camping together. They were on one hell of a shoestring budget; they had travelled all the way from the east coast in a shitty Toyota Hiace camper van with six surfboards strapped to the roof and a box of beans and spaghetti under their mattress. Their dinner each night consisted of boiled pasta with a sauce of peanut butter and soy sauce: satay spaghetti – delicious! It just goes to show that money doesn't decide how amazing your trip will be. They were also a bit lost when it came to fixing things, so I helped them get their interior lights going and showed them a thing or two about their camper van.

One of the highlights of my time around Perth was that I got to catch up with my brother Noy. He had flown over to meet his biological father and the rest of our extended family. We spent a few days adding another 20 or so members to our crazy, confusing family tree, and getting to know everyone. Family is something that is very important to both of us, so making those connections meant a lot. It was great to see my little brother finding answers to so many questions in his life.

From Perth I headed west up the coast. I stopped in at Kalbarri National Park, hiked a gorge and took some photos, but I had grown up in the Pilbara region of WA so it all looked very familiar to me, and besides, I was on a mission: I now had the westernmost point of Australia in my sights.

Steep Point was out on a very long peninsula of Shark Bay, and to get there, you had to cross endless sand dunes. For some strange reason I had expected this westernmost point to be some kind of tourist attraction. As I drove up the coast I tried to find out as much as I could about it but there wasn't much on YouTube or the net on what to expect.

The night before the big day I parked in a patch of desert scrub near a roadhouse. I googled dirt bike tips and tricks endlessly – amazingly, I had perfect reception. I stood up and imagined myself on the bike, leaning backward and forward, squeezing the tank with my legs. That night I tossed and turned endlessly.

The next morning, I checked into the Hamelin Pools Caravan Park, the last place to stop before setting off for the Point, and prepared as best I knew how. I had just over 160 km to ride in order to get to the tip, and I really didn't know what to expect. I wrote the following formula, which was to become my 'go to' list every time I prepped for a trip from that moment on:

Objective: to get to the westernmost point of the country.

Risks: death, injury, get lost, breakdown, dehydration.

Countermeasures: take first aid kit, use maps, take tools

or be prepared to walk out, take lots of water, eat lots of food

before going, ride slow.

   Worst-case scenario:

   Back-up plan:

   What's holding you back then?

I was starting to get comfortable with the feeling of fear. I would close my eyes and take deep breaths, and envision myself standing out on the edge of the continent. I knew the risks were high. I did all I could to prepare myself to be safe out there – death and injury were real threats. Plan, plan, plan. But if it all fell apart, I knew I was prepared to suffer those consequences.

I packed an overnight bag, enough canned food to see me through a few days, and a 10-litre fuel can. I sculled down about two litres of water and packed another five.

Riding out from the caravan park I was literally shaking. I had never ridden on corrugations before, and now I was riding over 100 km into the desert on sand dunes! What the hell!

I rode until my fuel tank ran dry, refuelled and stashed my remaining fuel in the bush. I figured I had enough to get me there and back to this point.

Before I knew it, the first sand dune was upon me. I leaned back on my little bike and ripped the throttle on. The bike screamed back at me and bumped and bounced all over the place like an angry bull before eventually running up the bank and getting sucked back down into the unforgiving sand. I had progressed about 20 metres. Stubborn and thick-headed, I pushed my bike to the top of that dune with roosters of sand flying out the back. By the time I got to the top, I was sucking in air like I was having a heart attack. The sweat was pouring from every pore in my skin. I sat on the sand and drank my precious water like a drug addict, the morning sun beating down on me. It was over 35 degrees.

From the top of the dune the view was pretty special in both directions. Behind me I could see the beautiful waters of Shark Bay, where I'd been last night; in front of me was an endless sea of rolling sand dunes.

I was in way over my head. I hadn't seen a car in over 100 km. *Turn back, Benji,* said that fearful voice in my head. *You shouldn't be out here. You're going to get yourself killed.*

Brundin! the other voice kicked in. You've still got a lot of legs left in you! Get to the next dune and assess from there! Keep going!

I got to the next dune, and then the next, and after a while, I started to get the hang of this sand-riding gig. It really was baptism by fire. The corrugations in the track were like mountains all lined in a row. It didn't take me long to figure out that I had to wrap the throttle on and just hold on and let the bike bounce across the tops. Eventually the track started to firm up and I found myself having the time of my life as I bounced over the endless corrugations and up and over the dunes.

I finally met another car at around the 140-kilometre mark. That was a relief but after a quick meet-and-greet, I left him in a cloud of dust and continued my journey west. As I rode on, it dawned on me that I was going to make it – I was going to f#@king make it!

The ocean came into view and the track hardened into rocky coral. A little pole held into the ground by a ball of concrete declared 'Steep Point'. I could not believe that I was here. Me!

I parked my bike and walked out to the cliffs. I can't tell you the elation I felt. The sense of achievement at overcoming the odds was exhilarating. *We made it! Hahaha!! Who would have thought?* "Benji, you're a f#@king legend!" I stated proudly into my GoPro camera.

Now, here is the funny thing. I had never thought of myself as an addict. My dad had been an alcoholic and would drink beer for breakfast if he could. The rest of my immediate family all suffered from addictions of some sort. But not me – no. When I was young, I would hyper-focus on being the fittest in the footy team instead of doing drugs. Then I focused on being the fittest in my navy dive squad, or the best at work. Whatever I did was always at the extreme end of that activity. When I was a boxer, I would shadow box in my sleep and watch endless hours of tutorials. At times, Scarlett would be having a conversation with me and she would catch me shadow boxing in my mind and walk off, frustrated. During the divorce process I got into the booze a lot more but I had still never thought of myself as an addict... maybe as a guy with an addictive personality. But let me tell you, at that western end of the world, the feeling I got, that euphoria, had me hooked.

The ride back through the dunes to the caravan park started tough. Having kicked back for a while to enjoy my success, my muscles had already begun to stiffen up. I'd ridden further than I had ever ridden in my life, and now I had to go all the way back. At one point I came off, got up and tried to start off again, only to lose the front wheel again almost immediately. I just didn't have the strength left to hold the bike up and had to let if fall onto me; I saw it falling in slow motion and lay on the ground, breathing hard, trying to compose myself.

When I finally rode my bike back into the caravan park, I grabbed a beer and went over to sit in the pool with some fellow travellers.

"Hey, mate, saw you take off this morning. Did you go up to Monkey Mia?" Dave and his wife Kerri were halfway through their trip across the country with their young daughter, Lila. He was a pretty fit guy and had ridden dirt bikes his whole life.

"I just got back from Steep Point." I was exhausted but smiling from ear to ear.

"You went out there all by yourself? Man, you've got some balls, mate, some bloody balls!"

"You don't know the half of it – I can't even ride a motorbike!"

Dave was awesome, and so were his wife and daughter. He showed me a thing or two about my bike, and also showed me his EPIRB (Emergency Position Indicating Radio Beacon) and how it worked.

"You need to get one of these, mate. As you go north, it just gets more and more remote. If you're going to do crazy shit like this, you're going to need one of these!"

I bought one as soon as I got into the next major town.

I left the Hamelin Pools Caravan Park the next day and went up to Monkey Mia. This was the place people raved on about because you got to feed the dolphins. But when I got there, all I saw was lines of tourists sitting around on banana lounges. And when it was time to feed the dolphins, there would be queues of up to 100 tourists all trying to get their bit of fish in. I took one look and did a U-turn. I was learning that this trip wasn't about the tourist attractions; it was about healing and pushing my limits.

I did, however, meet an American guy in the car park of the

Monkey Mia resort. We got chatting and the next thing we were in convoy together. Ethan was great. He was doing the west coast solo, but I don't think he had allowed for the incredible distances he would have to travel each day.

We spent a few days camping at a ruggedly beautiful place called Red Bluff, a little off the normal tourist road. We fished off the rocks and he caught the biggest of the day. Neither of us were at all good fishermen, but the fish were literally jumping at our hooks every time we cast them. It was a real rush. We ate sea bream for breakfast that day.

One afternoon we were sitting in our camp drinking a few beers and watching the sun set, and reflecting on the day. We had caught fish, gone exploring, swum in the ocean, and I had gone out on a pretty awesome bike ride across the cliffs of the West Australian coastline where herds of wild goats had run alongside me.

"Dude, this has been freakin' awesome, man! Could this day get any better?"

Just then two beautiful backpacker girls wearing bikinis walked up to our camp.

"Hello, lads, do either of you know how to fish?"

"Funny you ask. Ethan here is almost a pro." I smiled my best smile, sat back in my chair, took a swig of my beer and let my mate take the lead. We stayed up all night drinking and sharing stories around the fire. It was great to be alive.

From Red Bluff we continued north. Ethan had an 'oh shit' moment when his little hire car ran out of fuel on the side of the road. He got out of his car and ran down the highway waving wildly at me. Can you imagine it? Stuck on the side of the road in the middle of nowhere, watching your mate driving away over the horizon. It was five minutes or more before I noticed he was missing from my rear view. He was sure glad when I appeared back over the horizon.

We eventually went our separate ways. Ethan continued to Exmouth while I headed to Karratha to meet my cousin who was joining me for the journey through the Kimberley.

The Ride To Steep Point:
https://www.youtube.com/watch?v=iK3vxAWVGWM&t=253s

BB – KEY #3: MAKE A PLAN TO ACHIEVE YOUR GOAL.

Now that you have announced your goal and you understand your why, you need to make a plan!

Just start, even if you have no idea how the hell it's all going to come together. I knew I wanted to touch the compass points but I had no idea how that was going to happen. One step leads to another, so…

Break your plan into smaller, more manageable stages. They might be time periods or tasks, it's up to you. When I was in the deserts, I broke my days down into hours and even sand dunes. *Five more dunes, Benji, then you get to rest.*

The more details your plan has, the better. The more specifically you write down exactly what it is you want, and the more clearly you visualise that, the greater your chances of success. Vision boards have really helped me in the past. If you haven't made one in the past, a vision board is a poster with pictures and key words of what you want to experience. Many people cut the pictures and words out of magazines but you can also draw or mind map your vision, or make lists, or build it digitally. The how doesn't matter; just get it done.

Start with the big chunks and then keep chunking down to smaller and smaller details.

Chilling out inside my home

Bogged down in deep sand, Robe,SA

Coastline, Fitzgerald River National Park, WA

The westernmost point of Australia, Steep Point, WA

Camping at Red Bluff, WA

Red Bluff Sunset, WA

Chapter 5
THE KIMBERLEY

Life is either a daring adventure or nothing at all.

- Helen Keller

I first met Jasper many years ago in 2010 after tracking down my family in the Philippines. He was just a kid back then, barely nineteen. We had spent the better part of two weeks together, getting to know one another. I'd also had the chance to get to know the rest of the family deep in the jungles of the Philippines. It had been a very special time in my life. My relationship with Scarlett was still young then; we were in love and she was very supportive of me trying to put the pieces of my family tree together. Jasper had been the first relative to meet me and guide me into the Province. (He picked me up from the gates of a Filipino prison – but that's another story.) My younger brother Noy had come with me and together we put our mother's ashes to rest in the family lot with her other family members. It had been a dying wish of my mum to be laid to rest with her family, and I had been able to fulfil that wish for her, so it was quite an emotional time to be meeting our Filipino family.

Jasper had had a very hard childhood. At a young age, he'd started to get severe headaches, intense migraines and seizures that would cause him to pass out. After meeting with many doctors, the family had been advised that he had developed an inoperable brain tumour. There was nothing they could do but wait for the inevitable.

The family banded together and prayed for a miracle while their eldest son lay on his deathbed. It was a horrible time.

However, inexplicably, Jasper started to improve. The seizures stopped and, after a few years, there was no trace left of the terminal cancer in his brain. Jasper was given a second shot at life, and he embraced it with both hands. He went on to study Theology at university and became a pastor for his local church when he was in his early twenties. He devoted his life to God and the service of others. After a while, other churches would ask him to speak and tell his story at their church. His fame spread...

When we caught up, Jasper was in his late twenties and had travelled to over fifty countries. A gifted photographer, he has documented his adventures through some of the most remote parts of the world. He is a missionary for his church and has brought aid and faith to some of the poorest corners of the globe. He has a real passion for adventure – it was great to have him on board.

I picked him up at the Karratha Airport on a searing forty-degree Pilbara afternoon. The heat of that midday sun was enough to almost put me on my butt. I looked over at Jasper. To his credit, he didn't complain about it but the look on his face told me he was struggling. We had two weeks to get to Darwin, over 4000 km away;

not enough time to really appreciate the brilliance of the Kimberley.

We were both venturing into unknown territory. When I was 19, I had got as far as Karratha before turning back to Melbourne to care for my sick mother. Now, as we headed north from Karratha together, I couldn't help but think that Mum had something to do with my having family with me for this part of the journey.

We decided to make camp along the highway somewhere. Jasper was keen to get his cameras out as I had told him how spectacular the Pilbara nights could be. We drove off the beaten track a little until we came to a peaceful grove of trees. I parked on the high ground – it looked like a good spot to hang the hammock and set up camp. But Jasper pointed to another spot in the lowest part of the dry hollow we had found. "We'll see the Milky Way when it comes up better from here."

I checked the ground; despite being a riverbed it seemed dry and firm enough so I started to drive in… and felt my front wheels sinking. Shit! I backed up but was almost immediately bogged. "Shit, shit, shit!" What a way to start a road trip with your Filipino cousin!

I spent the next few hours, as the darkness crept in around us, frantically trying to hand-winch my home out of the riverbed. I had to set and reset my straps over and over, as well as unload everything out of my van to reduce the weight. I was chasing a falling sun when I said, "Jasper, sit here! If this strap breaks, whatever you do, don't let the van roll back. Got that? Make sure you put your foot on the brake immediately."

"Okay, sure, Ben. No problem. Is something very wrong?"

"No, mate, just keep your foot over that brake." His next comment floored me.

"Okay, sure. Just one question, Ben – which one is the brake?"

Finally, by some miracle, we were out and onto the firm stuff. The sweat was pouring from me. Jasper was having the time of his life watching this real outback adventure unfold, filming it all and asking me questions the whole time.

"Why are you digging this hole here, and why can't we just go backwards? Why can't we just call someone for a push?"

We drove back to within a few hundred metres of the road and started to walk all of our gear back to the van. Now that it was over, we could look back and laugh.

And then the stars started to come out.

If you have never been in the desert at night, let me tell you, you are missing out on one of the most brilliant displays Mother Nature can put on. The stars shine so brightly they completely light up the moonless night and you get a clear view of where you're walking, even in the bush, which is usually very dark at night. The sky is so big that you can see the arc of the world across the horizon. The kaleidoscope of colours is breathtaking.

Jasper was speechless. We sat on the roof rack and enjoyed the brilliant skyscape together.

From the Pilbara we ventured north-east up to Broome. We were pressed for time so only spent one afternoon there but watched possibly one of the best sunsets in Australia at Cable Beach. Jasper took some incredible shots that would later be used by National Geographic. And I rode my bike at full speed up the northern end of the beach. Hey, just another beach! Whatever.

We stopped into Lake Argyle where, again, Jasper took some incredible shots. This time I spoke with the camp managers and was able to negotiate free meals and accommodation for the two of us for three days in exchange for some pretty impressive shots of their infinity pool and lake. They got to use the shots in their advertising and promotional material, I got to ride around the lake on my motorbike and eat steak for breakfast, and Jasper got to explore and take some photos of some of the wildest parts of Australia. Between the two of us, we were having a ball.

We drove down the top end of Gibb River Road and stayed a few nights at El Questro Station. From there, we explored the many gorges and waterfalls in the area. It is incredible how you can drive through one of the most arid parts of the country and then come across a beautiful freshwater oasis in the heart of it all.

The Gibb River Road boasts an iconic river crossing, the Pentecost River. It has a rocky bottom and stretches about 200 metres from bank to bank. Although it was a little out of our way, I couldn't leave the Kimberley without at least going to have a look. I'd never crossed a river before, so I did some YouTube research and practised river crossings again and again at the front gates of El Questro where the Pentecost is only twenty metres wide and much more shallow. There are a dozen other little rivers and streams around the place that I threw my bike into just for good measure.

We left El Questro and drove the 30-odd kilometres back south along the Gibb River Road to where the Pentecost crosses its path. As we were pulling up, I saw two beady eyes and a set of nostrils submerge back into the murky depths.

"Shit! There's a croc sitting right there!"

"Where?"

We drove right up to the water's edge to the exact spot I had seen the eyes, but the crocodile had disappeared completely.

"It's okay. It was only a little freshwater one. I'm sure of it."

"How can you tell, Ben?"

"The snout was too narrow to be a salty."

"But how could you see it —?"

"Oh, I definitely saw it. Definitely…"

Jasper set his cameras up; he wasn't going to miss an opportunity like this to get a few stunning shots.

I pulled my bike off and got my gear on. I can tell you now, I was pretty bloody nervous. At that stage I hadn't yet spent enough time in the tropics to have developed a real respect for crocodiles, but seeing this one already had me second-guessing this whole bloody adventure. I felt ready to pull the pin on all of it.

This is what we signed up for, Brundin. Best to get on with it! There was that little voice again.

I hit the river in second gear, with a fair bit of momentum behind me. Suddenly the water was up over my front wheel. The rocky bottom pulled my wheel left and then right. I knew that if I put my legs down, they would act like big rudders and pull the bike sideways, even further off my line to the opposite bank. The water was splashing back up over the dash, into my face and visor, blocking my vision. I kept the throttle open and bumped my way into the shallow middle of the river. This was the point of no return. I regained my balance and pushed forward again into the deep stuff. The motor strained and revs gave way to gurgling as it sank into the water.

But little Whiskey just kept on trotting along. I was beginning to develop a real appreciation for what an amazing little bike I had been blessed with. Before I knew it, I was over to the other side. I fist-pumped the air in celebration. I had made it on my first go!

"Ben!" Jasper was yelling instructions from the far bank like a Hollywood director. "Ben! Can you hear me, Ben!"

"What's up, mate?"

"We have to do it again! I didn't get the shot I wanted."

"*What*!"

I rode back across again. Miraculously, I stayed upright.

"No, no! You have to do it again from *this* side, so it all flows the same way."

"Are you kidding me?" I was getting frustrated but I gritted my teeth and took off again.

On the second crossing, I dropped my bike in the middle. I somehow managed to keep the airbox out of the water and it didn't drown. But there I was, in the middle of the croc-infested Pentecost River, with water coming in over the top of my boots. You have never seen a guy turn a bike around and push it back to dry ground so fast in your life. I didn't know the human body was capable of moving that fast.

"Maybe we should call it a day, Jasper. I mean, we got a good run the first time. If I drop my bike out there again, I could drown it. Mate, I'm feeling pretty stuffed after that last try."

"It's okay, Ben, we can do it one more time and get an awesome shot, or we can just quit now and go home with nothing. I mean, really, I thought you weren't the quitting type. But it's okay; I mean, it's your bike…"

"*I'm not a quitter!*"

Jasper shrugged his shoulders and walked off. We ended up doing it again… and again.

From there we headed north to Lake Argyle. We met a whole heap of young British lads and German girls who were travelling in the same direction as us, and we ended up car-pooling with them all the way to Darwin: in total, six cars in convoy. They were aged between nineteen and twenty-five, and on the adventure of a lifetime. It was great to take photos with them and share our stories. In the evenings we set camp together and passed the nights playing cards and listening to music. I was glad that Jasper got to experience outback camping with a good bunch of fellow adventurers. We hiked into the Katherine Gorge and Edith Falls together before eventually parting ways.

Jasper and I finally arrived in Darwin after twelve days on the road together. It was an awesome leg of the whole journey for me. We had long talks about life, religion and the purpose of everything. We got on each other's nerves and had some tense moments under the stress of crocodiles, but overall, we got to know each other and developed a healthy respect for one another. I still speak to Jasper quite regularly and keep tabs on all of his adventures. He continues to travel and has taken some breathtaking shots all across the world: Africa, Peru and Norway, to name a few. One day I'm sure we will team up again to embark on another adventure.

BB – KEY #4: BUILD A TEAM.

When you have a goal, when people see that you have a purpose and direction, they will help you achieve it. People will come into your life to help you because that is how the universe works. Jasper, Vic, the blue carpet, the van… the universe has a plan. So just start doing whatever inspires you. If you start taking action and you announce to the world that this is what is going to happen, then people and things will come into your life that will enable you to make those things happen.

Friends encouraged me to keep going, to push myself into the wild places, and they revelled in the successes I had every time I shared a new story with them. No one gets to the top alone. And if they do, they're very lonely.

So start telling people what you are aiming to achieve! Yes, I know that takes guts and right now you're thinking, 'No way – people will laugh!' And they might. But those people are either extremely worried about you or they are stuck in inertia and not acting on *their* dreams, so you need to ignore anyone who isn't supporting you or is challenging you in a useful way. And keep your goals in sight.

So, tell me again, what are you going to do?

What have you done so far to achieve it?

And what markers have you put in place to

keep you accountable?

You need an accountability buddy.

Who is this going to be?

Pilbara nights

Lake Argyle infinity pool

Crossing the Pentecost River into El Questro Station

Gibb River Road, The Kimberley

Crossing the Pentecost River, Gibb River Road

Down time on Gypsy lane, Jasper editing photos, me servicing my bike

Success – the weary travellers arriving in the Northern Territory

Jasper cooking Filipino breakfast in the Australian outback

Chapter 6
KAKADU

You have to respect country.
We are all from the land, we share the land.
One day, we will go back to the land.
- Some old black fella I gave a lift to

When we got to Darwin, we treated ourselves to a nice hotel with a hot shower and a swimming pool. By then it was the weekend before Anzac Day and I had spent nearly eight weeks on the road.

Jasper flew back to the Philippines to continue his adventures, and I had a week to get myself ready for a mediation with my big nasty builder. I felt confident that this was the meeting that was finally going to resolve my ongoing building headaches. I had all of my facts and paperwork in order; the evidence against them was compelling. There was no chance they could look the other way when confronted with all this.

How wrong I was. The phone conference was a disaster: they denied liability over every single thing I threw at them. I was in shock.

"In a way this is good news, Ben," the mediator said. "What this means now is that we can issue a certificate of non-resolution and you can start legal proceedings."

Oh, great! Another year of this bullshit.

Darwin is a party town. In April and May the backpackers start to pour in. It's the start of the dry season so the weather is as good as it gets. A friend of mine flew up from Melbourne to see me and we went out and painted the town red. We had a lot of fun, but I was still fragile, and a pub or nightclub was the last place I wanted to be. After a week in Darwin, I knew I had to get out of there.

I had left Melbourne with Darwin in my sights. Darwin had been the top of the mountain for me. And now that I was here, I didn't know what to do. I was feeling lost again and back to the start. *What the hell am I going to do with my life?* This was the question rolling around in my head once again.

I asked this question out loud more than once. I even scribbled it in my note pad with a giant question mark: *What the hell am I going to do now?*

I didn't know what I was going to do with my life, but I decided I'd head out to Kakadu for a few days to clear my head and ride my bike around. I thought three days would be enough to see the whole place, surely. So I packed my van and left Darwin.

When I arrived in Kakadu, I decided to stay at a resort that had been recommended to me as it was right in the heart of the national park. I won't identify it here, but for fun we'll call it Welcome Waters.

It was late in the day so I parked and went straight to the bar to get a beer. A young guy was working there and we started chatting.

Next thing I knew, I was being introduced to the human resources person, and, it just so happened, the general manager was also on the scene. After a quick chat with him, I suddenly had a job working in the maintenance department. Like that, the universe had answered my question.

The GM shook my hand, saying: "Welcome to the jungle, mate." But he was smirking as he said it. He knew something I didn't, but I was absolutely about to find out.

I had a week before I started so I decided to head back to Darwin, tie up some loose ends and grab some supplies. I was pumped! I now had work lined up, so I didn't have to worry about money. Driving out of the park, I came across a broken-down old Holden Commodore on the side of the road. Lying around it, under the shade of the trees, were six older indigenous guys. They had taken the flat tire off and were now just waiting for someone to come along.

I pulled up next to them with a big grin on my face. "Hey lads, what's up? Need any help?"

One of the guys lifted his hat from his face and looked up at me, irritated and suspicious: why would this fella stop and start a conversation? Usually the white tourists just shot on past.

I got out and introduced myself. To break the ice, I opened my back door and showed the men my fridge.

"Oh... hey bloke, you got any beer in there?"

"No beer, brother, but how about some water?"

Turns out they were heading to the local roadhouse for supplies when their car got a flat. The local roadhouse was over 100 km in the other direction but I offered to drive one of them there to get another tire.

Dimitri and I finished off the last of my orange juice on the way. Once he had established that I was a good fella, he just would not stop talking about his land and his people; I told him about my job and where I'd be working. By the time we got to the roadhouse, we were like old friends.

A few weeks later, when I was working at the bar, guess who happened to be there? Turns out Dimitri and his friends were some of the traditional owners of the lands. So guess who was invited to go out exploring in some of the most remote and untouched regions of Kakadu?

Kakadu is the largest national park in Australia. It's located about 200 km from Darwin and stretches almost 200 km north to south and over 100 km east to west. It covers an area of over 20,000 square km. Shaped like a giant playing card, it has a huge escarpment wall that stretches from the Katherine Gorge in the south all the way up into Arnhem Land in the north. This wall is a sheer vertical cliff, stretching over 200 metres high in some areas. Most of Kakadu was under a shallow sea nearly 150 million years ago, with the escarpment wall adopting the role of giant immovable sea cliffs.

Up on the escarpment wall, more commonly known as the Stone Country, the land is harsh and dry. Huge crevasses open up under foot as the water of a million years of flood and rain has washed away much of the topsoil, leaving the stony plateau barren and dry. Creeks have cut huge gorges in the soft stone, leaving pockets of dense monsoonal rainforest, protected, by the shadow of the wall, from the harsh tropical sun. Dozens of waterfalls cascade off this wall into the rivers and creeks below. Some run dry in the hotter months, while in the peak of the wet season they can produce their own cloud systems high above.

Kakadu is also the only national park in Australia that is home to an entire river system. The South Alligator runs from its source in the Stone Country to the coast in the north. It is one of the most densely populated rivers in the world – with big estuarine crocodiles.

Below the escarpment wall stretch the endless floodplains, as far as the eye can see. These flood plains cover almost 70% of the entire park. In the wet season, most of Kakadu is under water as the monsoonal rain floods over the escarpment wall like the raging torrent of a burst river dam.

I had arrived in Kakadu at the start of the dry. Each week the floodwaters receded further, leaving a network of billabongs and an abundance of flora and fauna to explore.

Here is another fun fact: the whole world's water quality is measured by the Stone Country. Up on the plateau there is no human impact – no farming, mining or agriculture to pollute the quality of the water for thousands of kilometres – so the water here is used as the benchmark to test all freshwater river systems around the world.

Kakadu is also home to the oldest practising culture in the world. You can walk through the Stone Country and along the escarpment wall and find rock art everywhere. Rock art depicting thylacines (Tasmanian tigers) has been dated at up to 65,000 years old. There are over 280 bird species alone in the park, many of which migrate there to breed during the dry season, and over 70 species of mammals and 117 species of reptiles, including freshwater and saltwater crocodiles. Buffalo, pigs and horses run wild in the park; it isn't uncommon to see them walking along the highway.

Kakadu is a World Heritage-listed site for both cultural and natural universal values; only four other sites hold both titles in Australia. It is rich with history, culture and wildlife. It is rugged and isolated – literally cut off from the rest of the world. It is the wildest place in all of Australia. It is beautiful. It was to be my home for the next four months. And Welcome Waters was the perfect place to set up base and plan countless expeditions on my bike into the great wild unknown.

1 July 2018

Dear Everyone,

I hope you guys have all been well.

I know how busy we all are, and my phone and internet reception are pretty poor to say the least up here. If the park is full, I can't even check Facebook because the signal jams up. And if I'm more than 5 km from the actual resort, my phone reception is non-existent. So I thought I would write this old-fashioned letter just to touch base and give you all some updates.

I can remember last year asking the universe for an adventurous life. I can tell you now, it has delivered in spades! I've been here for just on two months and have fallen in love with this place.

Tourists who visit really only get to see about 10% of the park because most of it is hidden away and out of reach to the public. I'm getting to know a lot of the traditional owners – just the other day, I was invited to ride my bike around a huge billabong teeming with wildlife. I was the only person out there; I had nothing but my bike and a beacon. It was incredible!

I do have to be careful how I ride, though. You have to expect that a buffalo will be waiting around every thicket, so I've started practising evasive manoeuvres. I can take my bike from top gear, put it into a controlled skid and slide, gear down and have it belting back the other way in about five seconds. I still can't mono or do jumps but I can hold a pretty good line on some pretty chewed-up roads at about 100 km an hour.

I feel like I have so many adventures to tell you all about, and I do mean to write them all down, but it seems that no sooner one has finished, than another one is beginning!

For instance, last weekend I rode my bike out to a huge waterfall 100 km away and met a base jumper there. We hiked to the summit the next day and he showed me how to climb down into the top pool – and then he jumped off.

I suddenly found myself all alone in one of the most remote parts of the most remote part of Australia. I only had about two hours of sun left and had to navigate my way back down using nothing but the sun, rocks and trees to get a bearing. I did get lost and had to calm my nerves a few times. I had water, a knife and a lighter, so shelter wasn't going to be an issue. However, when I finally got down again, I had to ride my bike back to our rendezvous point in the dark to meet up with some girls. Which was pretty hairy, seeing the place is full of buffalo.

Over the course of that particular weekend I rode my bike over 500 km. Three hundred of that was on the pegs[2] through some pretty rough roads.

One day I got back from a morning ride with only fifteen minutes to spare before I started my arvo shift and my postie bags held on with cable ties and electrical tape. Later that day, hobbling through the resort on buckled legs, eyes the colour of shiraz from all the dust, I couldn't help the big cheesy grin on my face. Some guests asked why I was so happy, and I told them of the adventures I have out here. They loved it!

I have been having the time of my life. I can't remember ever feeling so wild and reckless and free. My dopamine levels must be through the roof! I've been training again and have started running a few mornings a week with one of the older guys I work with. He wants to be able to run 5 km without stopping, so I said I'd help him get there. I also hung a heavy bag from a tree and convinced the operations manager that it would be a good idea to buy some boxing gear so I could run some classes for those who are interested. It's been heaps of fun.

I feel like I am constantly running on empty but keep finding more energy. It's like I'm twenty-one again – no one here can believe I'm actually twenty-nine![3]

How can you explain this place in a letter? Just yesterday morning after a run, I walked down to the billabong to have

---

2   Standing in the saddle.
3   I was actually thirty-four but none of the suckers there needed to know that!

a quick fish and there was a huge four-metre croc in my spot. I had to throw rocks at him to get him to go away and then flicked my line in anyway. That is just so normal here.

While I write this letter, I'm chilling in my hammock and watching the bowerbirds build their nest; the male is now courting the female. I can't leave any cutlery out, because they steal it and put it in their nests.

This place is undoubtedly the wildest place I've ever been. Wild mobs of buffalo run along the highway, pigs and brumbies run across open flood plains while you flick a line for barramundi, dingoes stalk me while I run in the dawn, crocs sit on the banks of the rivers and billabongs with their mouths gaping open, and countless birds and reptiles fill the trees and the sky. Out here, nature really calls the shots, and I am constantly reminded of that.

I end up drinking beers with the staff and new friends I've met here most nights, and when I get a few days off, I just can't wait to get my gear on and head off into the wild places. I finally get my bike spares this weekend so I'll rebuild it over the coming days. I can't wait!

7 July 2018

Turns out my impatience has got the better of me once again. I went riding last weekend before my spares came in and the nuts on my exhaust mount shook loose and snapped my muffler clean off. Rode back to the resort with the straight pipe roaring like a Harley. Further inspection showed that my stretched chain has chewed into the swing arm and down into the swing arm bearings. An expensive lesson to learn, and now I'll be out of action for at least four weeks while I try to get it to Darwin for repair!

Met another tour guide during the week, though, and managed to snatch a spot on a chartered flight to Cobourg this week, so that's good news.

How is everything back home? I do miss you all. Hope to be back in Melbourne around January for some summer fun. (I still can't surf, by the way...)

Gotta go now, I know we are all busy so please just send my love to everyone and tell them I'm thinking of them all.

Take care,

Love Benji.

Kakadu snapped me in like the powerful jaws of a saltwater crocodile. It sucked me down and took me in deep to the very heart of its soul. And I wrapped my arms around its giant reptilian head and held on for dear life.

The resort itself was huge, with powered camping for over 800 people, lodge rooms for an additional 200, permanent camp kitchens and tents for the numerous touring companies that would frequent the park, three swimming pools, a full bar, stage, kitchen, grounds, gardens, an airfield and light aircraft, to say nothing of the fleet of cruise boats and six huge four-wheel-drive tour buses. We pumped our own water from the escarpment. Three huge generators powered the whole place; we burned through over 1200 litres of diesel a day! We processed our own sewerage. We even had a little store that sold groceries, fuel and bits and pieces. There was a live-in staff of over 110 people in the peak of the dry season.

I started working the morning shift in the maintenance department and was the youngest by at least 30 years. The other men who made up the team were all retired blokes who enjoyed the laid-back semi-retired life of resort living. That said, we had our hands full! We were tasked with maintaining the whole resort, as well as anything else that popped up. My job changed every day from watering the grass to fixing broken doors to reversing caravans for guests.

On my second day, a back-burning fire got out of control and the wind started to pick up and turn it toward the resort. Before I knew it, my friend Lewis and I and the brave few of the maintenance department, the retired old war dogs, were filling the water tankers and rushing off to save the airfield. I was right into it, my bandana tied up around my face to filter the smoke. I kept wetting my clothes to help combat the heat of the flames. The hair on my arms singed down to nothing and my throat was coarse from the smoke but I was having the time of my life running up and down the airfield, trying to get ahead of the front.

A few months later I was having a beer with the operations manager and we spoke of that day. He and the general manager had been in Darwin. They kept getting reports on their phones about the fire and were pulling their hair out. "What the hell are the new staff doing out there! Have they even had training? This is a public liability nightmare!"

It was true. We shouldn't have been out there. But if not us, then who? There was no fire department, no emergency services. It just rammed home for me how truly isolated we were. We had to be totally self-sufficient in everything we did. Outside of the resort, the wild flood plains of Kakadu stretched for 100 km in every direction.

That night, once the fire was under control, I worked my first shift on the bar. I loved being able to interact with the guests. We were all travelling and we were all excited to be there. People were in a good mood and I loved to chat.

I met two beautiful girls who were having a break from their busy lives in NSW. We got chatting and when I finished my shift I took one out to do some astro-photography on the still-smoking airfield. They ended up staying another two nights.

A few days later, on my day off, I was eating my lunch in the staff mess when a two-metre king brown snake decided she wanted lunch too. The French guy I was sitting with turned grey in the face when he saw it slither in. Having spent a part of my childhood in a zoo as the snake handler's assistant, I watched with interest as a few of the older chefs, who had their snake-handling certificate, were called in to deal with it. The whole ordeal started to draw a crowd, and at one point I had to forcibly push one of the Malaysian workers back as he was trying to film the snake with his iPhone even while it lashed out at us!

Catching that snake was a moment I will never forget. We finally had it cornered in the toilet cubicle when it lashed out at the chef who had the hook and bag. The poor guy threw the kit at the snake and jumped back to save himself. I grabbed the bag and snake tongs and took over his position.

The snake found its way into the hollow interior of a steel door jamb. I was immediately up on the walls, ripping panelling apart to make sure it couldn't get into the exposed roof cavity. Once we determined it was trapped, we decided to flush it out with water. Dave, one of the guys from Maintenance, drilled a 22-millimetre hole into the top of the jamb and pushed a garden hose into the opening. Within minutes, the whole mess and toilets were flooded. The general manager started alternately banging on the door jamb with a broom stick and whispering encouragement to the furious snake within. He had big problems with snakes living around his house and had a real hatred of them.

We had forgotten that we were the respectable staff of a world-class resort; we were suddenly wild with the hunt. The damage to the floor, the walls and the door meant little. We had the taste of the hunt in our mouths: man versus beast. My heart was pumping as I crouched only inches from the hole in the jamb that the snake had crawled into. It started to poke its head out for breath then shot back into the 'safety' of the flooding jamb. All the while, the general manager was banging away, enraging it even further. Dave was wriggling the hose and adjusting the pressure. The Frenchies had come out to see the fuss, the chef was rolling a smoke and offering his two-bob worth, and Malaysia was still hovering over my shoulder with his iPhone.

"Okay, everyone, just stop, stop, *stop*! Be quiet and let it come out. This time I will get it."

The silence drew on for what felt like an eternity. Cautiously, the snake showed her nose, her forked tongue flicking in and out, trying to pick up her hunters' scent. Everyone was holding their breath.

I sat like a statue, my prongs poised, ready to strike.

The snake ventured out that little bit further. She turned her head slightly and looked straight at me, straight into my eyes. She was locked on; her prey had been found. I had seen snakes with that look in their eye before. I had watched king browns and taipans and tiger snakes stalk their prey. This snake was stalking me. Her furious anger was being turned on me. I was the cause of all her stress and discomfort. Did I not know who the hell she was? She was the deadliest hunter in the land, feared by all. Who the hell was I to disrupt her day so?

I dared not break eye contact with her. Her forked tongue flicked again. In my mind, I could see her body in the door jamb, coiling like a spring, ready to strike. All I needed was another centimetre of neck and I'd have her. Her eyes were hypnotic. Her neck peeled out of the jamb, ever so slowly. The distance between us closed, our eyes were less than a metre apart.

Snap! I shot in with the prongs and got a grip just behind her skull. Her mouth gaped open and venom shot from her loaded fangs.

I pulled her free of the door and stood there with a two-metre king brown in my hands. The adrenalin was like electricity, not just in me but in everyone. We put the beautiful snake in a drum, and Dave and Chef Rick drove out into the bush to release her back into the wild. I would have gone with them, but I had a waterfall to get to and the sun was falling. I grabbed my bag, scoffed my food, and was on my bike for another adventure.

All of that happened within a week of my arrival and set the tone for the next four months of my life. I never once watched a TV while I was in Country. I was always running on four to five hours sleep, yet somehow I kept finding the energy to keep going. When I look back at my time in Kakadu, there are just so many stories to tell.

And incredible people with whom such great memories were made.

Welcome Waters attracted all kinds of characters to work in the resort. Everyone had a story, and everyone was trying to get away from something: bad debt, broken homes, dark pasts. Management was made of an assortment of old and young employees, all either trying to further their careers in hospitality or also hide from something in their other lives.

The maintenance department was like the infantry of the park. The combined wealth of 'hands-on' practical knowledge they had accumulated over a lifetime meant that there was not a problem they couldn't solve, a structure they couldn't build, or a boat they couldn't fix.

The kitchen was run by a Scottish tyrant: in the heat of service he could be heard barking orders to the other chefs like a general on Braveheart's battlefields. The young chefs would obey his commands and whip up dish after dish of five-star cuisine. The food and beverage division was huge, and there were shopkeepers and bartenders. The housekeeping division had a small army of Chinese girls to keep the place shipshape.

The group of young pilot lads were all in their mid- to late twenties and all devilishly handsome. It was like there was this prerequisite to be a pilot: young, fit and well dressed with a comb-over haircut.

There was Sky Blue, the cross-dressing crackhead from Brisbane. Her alter ego, Shane, was a beer-swilling fella from the outback who liked to talk to the heterosexual men in a thick Aussie swaggering accent, while simultaneously trying to grope them. She loved to rouse a reaction out of them before laughing to herself in a high-pitched squeal and running off to find attention elsewhere.

And then there was toothless old Rick, the 'snake-handling' chef. I actually don't know how long he had been in the park. He was a quietly-spoken man, polite and kind and frail. He mustn't have weighed more than sixty-five kilograms. But once he had a few drinks in him, he could become loud and wild. One night, while stumbling back from the bar, he came across a family of tourists taking photos of and admiring cane toads. Rick launched into a run and took a swinging kick at the biggest toad, sending it ten metres into the air. The family sat there stunned, not knowing what to say. Rick took a drag of his cigarette and drawled, "They're a f#@king pest," before casually walking off.

There were the tour guides – hippies at heart, nurturers, environmentalists, animal activists. They were passionate, opinionated, animated and excited about their incredible job – at least, they were at the start of the season.

I was also lucky enough to meet and become friends with some of the local Indigenous people and traditional owners of the land. One night at the bar early in the season, one guy invited me to ride my bike around his family's lands. This system of rivers and billabongs wasn't open to the general public, so it was an opportunity to see some of the wildest, most untouched parts of Kakadu. When I asked how big these lands were, Brad smiled at me and said, "Lily Pond is about three-quarters of Kakadu."

Someone else who knew the area really well was Franko. He and his sons had been part of the land their whole lives. They worked bloody hard collecting seeds and plants in preparation for re-naturalising the areas damaged by the old mines. Quite often I would run into them in the maintenance yard.

"Benji, it's great to see you getting out and exploring this place," Franko would say. "There's so much to see here, and most of these other punters just don't take advantage of the opportunity they get. It's great to see you having a crack out there. Now listen, if you ever go down this end of the park," pointing to a location on the small map I carried around with me, "look for these big boulders. From there, you'll find a track. Follow that until you get to a river. Don't swim there, but hike up it for about two days, and you'll come to a waterfall..." Franko was always sending me out on the greatest adventures.

The Indigenous guys would also give me tips on places to go and things to get out and see. I was an A-grade student, making notes on everything they said and absorbing all of their advice. I loved it, and they loved sharing their beautiful lands with me and seeing my genuine excitement.

In the peak of the season, there were over 110 staff living on-site together. The staff had their own little village: portable buildings all lined in rows. I made some great friends in that place.

I opted to live out of my van in the campgrounds in order to save on rent; I figured it was the better option since I'd only be sleeping there. I found the best spot in the whole campground in among a huge half-moon-shaped garden with immense shady trees that would keep the heat out of my van. And I could swing my hammock from the tall palm trees. I tied ropes through all of the trees and hung huge tarps overhead like sails to stop the branches and foliage from falling into my camp.

The gardens that surrounded my van were made up of dense fern trees and undergrowth that acted as a natural barrier to the rest of the campgrounds. It was a small private oasis among the chaos of the caravaners' city. I had as much space as I could ever need, and more. My home was far away from the staff village, which afforded me privacy from the staff and management. I managed to commandeer a few of the bar stools from the restaurant and a bar table also. It was the perfect little camp.

Most nights after work, I'd have a few of the staff, the tour guides from other companies, or even some of the park guests back to Gypsy Lane for drinks. It became part of my daily routine to sneak the dozens of empty pint and wine glasses back to the kitchen without the chef or anyone else noticing. I giggled to myself every time I had to do this; it was like I was a naughty school kid.

One night I had Kerry, Dave and their daughter, the family I had met in Steep Point, camping for a few nights with me. The pilots came into our camp with a few boxes of beer, which we drank happily, laughing that one of the youngest pilots had to do the morning flight the next morning. Kerry and Dave laughed too, but made a mental note to do the sunset flight the next day!

Another night, all the tour guides from the other Territory tour companies came over with a few bottles of Jack Daniels; then the ladies from reception came down after they'd shut up for the night. "Oh, Benji we've heard so much about your little camp, we just had to come down and see what all the fuss was about." We had a hilarious evening. It was always fun to see new faces walking into camp with a tray of drinks. There was never a dull moment.

Eventually someone complained about the noise, and management had to enforce a noise curfew throughout the campgrounds. This was hilarious too, because the night manager was the worst offender of all for getting drunk and boisterous. On more than one occasion, I had to pull the pin on the evening drinks because *he* was getting too loud. If he was on the morning shift the next day, he'd find himself listening to the guests complain to him about the unruly noise that he himself had been making the night before…

The adventures just kept coming. Every day I would finish work and within twenty minutes, I would have my riding gear on, my pre-ride checks done, and I'd be out into the flood plains, venturing further and further afield. I felt the fear of venturing out alone before every ride, but I made sure I focused on everything that I could control. If something was going to happen to me out there, I just had to make sure I had planned and drilled for it as best I could. Even if I was only going out for an hour or so, I would always make sure someone knew what direction I was heading in.

After a few expensive lessons in bike maintenance, I began to make meticulous checks before every ride. I followed a very disciplined routine of checking my bike, checking my tools, my beacon, my water and my food. I loved the pre-ride bike checks as much as I loved the actual riding. I had brought structure and discipline back into my life, and I was taking ownership of my bike, and my life, once again.

I had to cross the South Alligator River on quite a few occasions. Knowing that the possibility of drowning my bike was likely, I drilled myself on how to undrown a motorbike and practised again and again taking the tank off and removing the spark plug. This saved my skin months later when I actually did drown my bike on the Creb Track in Far North Queensland. Had I not practised this skill,

I would never have known that I needed an extension bar on my socket to remove the spark plug. Not having that one bit of kit would have ended my adventure and left me stranded in the bush.

I also learnt that whenever I came across water, I needed to tune in, stay sharp, and roll through slowly. Where there is water, there is wildlife. This drill saved me one day when I came up to a herd of bullocks resting by the water's edge. They were as startled as me and ran up the bank and into the bush. Had I been going much faster, I would have almost parked on top of them.

Crocodiles were also a very real problem to consider. Having spent so much time around water by this stage, I'd developed a very healthy respect for these prehistoric dinosaurs. They can be completely invisible in only three feet of water.

They are cold creatures: they show no emotion, no remorse or fear. They simply have one purpose and that is to kill anything that comes within reach. Their mouths are full of giant razor teeth riddled with the rotting flesh of their past victims. Even if you were bitten by one of these creatures and managed to get away, the infection from the bite would make you incredibly sick if you didn't get immediate treatment. Their body is shaped like a giant bullet to help it cut through the water and close on their prey quickly. I have seen the enormous beasts grab pigs and disappear into the depths without so much as raising their pulse, the squeals of their prey turning into feeble gurgles. Crocodiles will twist their body and whip their head from side to side in order to tear their prey apart. They are an apex predator, designed to hunt, to close, to kill and destroy. They are magnificent killing machines. And they do not discriminate. People die every year in the top end from crocodile attacks.

So every time I came to a river crossing, the hair would be up on the back of my neck. I'd be hyper alert and feel two waves of fear come over me: one, that there might be buffalo by the water, and two, that there might be crocodiles in the water.

Pigs, on the other hand, are entertaining. One day I saw some pigs on the flood plain and chased them for ages on my bike, laughing at the fun of it like a schoolboy. The pigs suddenly changed their course and the ground turned into a swampy bog in front of me. I nearly went over the handlebars. I had to think quickly. I was almost 100 km from any main road, my bike was up to the forks in reeds and mud, and I was struggling to pull it backwards. The longer I splashed about in the water, the more likely a giant hungry lizard was making his way to my position. I jumped into the muddy water and heaved the front wheel up out of the sludge. Covered in stinking mud I continued on my ride, fist-pumping the air at yet another small victory. After that day, I had to acknowledge that if I was to continue riding out into the wilderness, the possibility of actually losing my bike in a bog or a deeper river was a real possibility. If that happened, I had to have anything I needed to survive out there strapped to my body, not my bike.

My new set-up was: beacon strapped to my body armour high on my chest; my first aid kit and Leatherman multi-tool attached to a belt on my hip; lighter, food rations, drone, three litres of water and a torch in my back pack; a whistle on my right wrist and a hunting knife duct-taped to the back of my riding boot. It had once been on my hip, but after a bad fall one day, it was ripped off, and I didn't like wearing hard objects I could fall onto around my waist.

On my actual bike, I strapped extra fuel if I needed it, a small hatchet, my toolkit with a spare tube and pump, an additional two litres of water, two cans of tuna and beans, my GoPros and spare batteries. These were kept wrapped in a plastic bag inside a cheap tank bag with a broken zip I'd bought on eBay for $30. I also sealed all my bandages, painkillers and antiseptics in snap-lock bags to prevent them from getting fouled in dirty river water.

And after seeing yet another huge snake while out on a ride one day, I made sure I kept a brand-new permanent marker at the top of my first aid kit. That way, should I get bitten by a snake out there, I could pressure-wrap the bite, flick my beacon on, and write a note on my forearm with all the details of what happened: name, time of bite, location, description of snake, etc. Then, if I passed out before anyone found me, at least they would know what happened. I figured the only thing worse than getting bitten by a snake in the middle of nowhere was not being prepared for it. And yes, some might think it was a shit plan, but a shit plan is better than no plan.

Adventures happened to me almost daily, certainly weekly. I would roll back into the resort and burst into the staff mess in full kit, covered in mud, dust and days of sweat, starving and beaming from ear to ear.

"Guys, you wouldn't believe what just happened! I crossed this river, and there was this crocodile and it had a wallaby in its mouth, and then I saw a herd of over fifty wild horses and a stallion reared up at me, and then there was this buffalo and it chased me. But I got away. And there was this flock of hundreds of birds and I chased them with my drone. And then the track was so bumpy the bike was just bouncing all over the place like this..." And I would re-enact the bike bouncing. "And then I found a waterfall and then this happened and that and...! What's for dinner? I'm starving. Have you guys eaten? Let's get a beer. What did I miss here? Who has tomorrow off? Let go out to this spot the traditional owners told me about. Who's keen?" The other staff would laugh at me, at how totally amped up I was, while I piled my plate full of food and kept on talking in between mouthfuls.

I loved being out there, pushing myself, planning for every type of worst-case scenario. I had no illusions that I was some incredible motorbike rider because I knew I wasn't; in fact, that knowledge is probably what kept me alive. I took my time. I wasn't in a rush to be anywhere or go at breakneck speed. I just loved pitting myself against the elements.

One day I was sitting with one of my friends and he asked me why I did it, why I threw myself out there so far and so hard.

"I spent the first thirty-four years of my life holding back, mate," I said. "Now it's time to really start living!"

I told him about my life, my divorce and how I'd ended up in Kakadu.

"A few years ago, when things were really down for me, I pleaded with the universe to give me an adventurous life. The universe was listening! It brought my van into my life, put a motorbike in my lap, and dropped me deep in the heart of the wildest place in Australia. When I was offered this job on top of all that, I just thought it would be rude not to take the universe's offer and really explore!"

"Shit, be careful what you wish for, hey? Don't you get scared out there?"

"Of course! I'm shitting my pants every time I get on the bike, but I think that's a good thing. If I went out there feeling cocky, I'd probably be dead by now. And every time something happens and I beat it, the feeling I get is just crazy. Every day that I don't die out there means I get to go out the next day and absolutely live it all over again!"

"But why motorbikes? What is it about riding?"

"When you drive a car, it's like you're watching a movie. When you're on the bike, it's like you're *in* the movie. When you ride on the beach, you can taste the salt air on your lips. When you're in the bush, you can feel the ground change through your handlebars. You feel the bush change before you see it. You're in tune with the world around you. You are one hundred per cent focused and present in that very moment in time. You feel the temperature change when you ride through a dip in the forest. You hear the motor working below you and see the shadows of the clouds move across the open flood plains in front of you. The hair stands up on the back of your neck and your eyes narrow when you smell the buffalo close at hand. I had never noticed that until I got on a bike. There is nothing quite like it in the world."

How could he argue with that?

The flood plains of Kakadu were like one giant training ground for me, and I treated them as such. For example, one day the track I was riding on suddenly fell away abruptly into a dry sandy riverbed. I hadn't expected such a sharp drop. I came off and rolled into the sand. I picked myself up and inspected the bush around me for a better spot to enter the riverbed. I proceeded to ride my bike in and out of the river a dozen times until I felt confident that, should I ever come across this track again, or something similar, I could traverse it comfortably.

My hunger for adventure was insatiable. I was always dragging someone along with me, or getting into some sort of mischief.

I had been shown the way to a secret waterfall by a base jumper I'd met on one of my adventures. The views from the top of those waterfalls had been simply breathtaking and I'd promised to take some of my friends back there to share in their brilliance. Finally the day came when Lewis, Ama and I would share a day off. After work, we sat at the bar and planned to head out the next morning at 7 a.m. I knew the hike into the falls was a tough one, so we all left the bar early to get a good night's rest.

No sooner had I walked back into my camp when I got a call from another friend, Cade.

"Benji, let's go fishing. I'll pick you up in five minutes!"

How could I say no?

After a few beers, we decided that it would be an adventure to forge our way through the system of billabongs and see how far we could get. The billabongs were teeming with crocodiles. I kept my Led Lenser torch beam shooting into the moonless night, looking for the next bottleneck in the banks of the billabongs. The red eyes of the crocs glared back at me. In some spots, the waterways got so narrow we had to use the oars to push the hanging pandanus leaves aside, always carefully checking them for tree snakes and orb spiders. It was past midnight before we finally came to a dead end, and almost 5 a.m. before I stumbled back into my camp. Two hours later, I had to get up and take Lewis and Amelie, or Ama, up into the Stone Country to find our way to a secret water hole.

Lewis was one of my closest friends during my time in Country. He was in his mid-twenties and had a similar passion for adventure.

He had grown up in the southern end of Western Australia and had decided to let go of his dreary university degree and travel the world instead. He had spent months living and travelling through South-East Asia, and managing a hostel in Thailand. Now he was a tour guide in Kakadu and could list off all the wildlife at a glance. Lewis loved to share his adventures and was a keen photographer. His Instagram page, Huntingforparadise, had over 15,000 followers. And rightly so – he took a pretty incredible photo.

Ama was a gypsy traveller from Boulder, USA. She had been a schoolteacher once but kicked that career in the butt when she realized what a pain in the arse kids were. She always had a story to tell, and they normally revolved around some guy she was seeing and the crazy things they got up to. She ended up moving down into the campgrounds with me and sleeping in her car. We joked that we were the hobos of Kakadu. She loved the wild places as much as Lewis and me, so it was no surprise that the three of us struck up a friendship.

We met at the bar just before seven. I was still red-eyed from the night before so just heaped a bag together with all my cameras, drone and water in it. I didn't think it through – the pack must have weighed over 15 kilograms. Lewis and Ama had to hitch a ride out to the escarpment, and I met them out there on my bike. By the time I had ridden the 100 km to join them, I was in no better condition; they laughed at my self-inflicted discomfort.

To add to the joke, Lewis helped me fix the straps on my bag while secretly adding his own three-litre water bottle to my pack. Climbing up the steep and rocky goat track to the top of the escarpment was challenging enough, even for someone sober, and I struggled. My clothes were drenched with sweat by the time we finally crested the last rise into the Stone Country.

The Stone Country is like walking into another world. Millions of years of flood and rain have cut huge crevasses into the stony plateau. The bush is dry, and coarse shrubs and trees cling to the rocky surface, their roots pushing deep into the rocks as they look for the last of the escaping water.

Ribbons that have been hung from the trees every 20-30 metres mark the track from the top of the escarpment wall to the top of the waterfalls. These ribbons are exposed to the elements all season, and over time become brittle, eventually falling off and disappearing. I had been up here once before and knew how easy it was to miss a ribbon.

At one point, we decided to take our chances and jump across a crevasse instead of trying to find a way around it. Lewis and I made it easily, but Ama, who was vertically challenged, almost didn't get across – Lewis had to grab her hand and pull her forward. We all laughed nervously.

"Wow, Ama, you almost didn't make that." Lewis remarked nervously.

"I know. I nearly died." She was right: the drop was almost ten metres into the void.

The waterfalls we had hiked to were a series of huge cascades: dozens of small steps in the main river above, and then three big waterfalls plunging into their own huge pools. The largest of these falls had a drop of over 187 metres.

Once we arrived at the top of the waterfalls, we searched around for a way to get down into the pools. We were well off the marked track, so there were no more ribbons directing our way. We were no longer tourists; we were adventurers, carving our own path through the wilderness, seeking the unknown, looking for a place that no man had ventured before us.

From the top of the stony plateau, we could see the twelve-metre waterfall plummeting into the pool below. I couldn't remember how I had gone in the last time I was here.

Lewis was as excited as a schoolboy. He ventured out to find the crack in the cliff face that would take us into the bottom pool. We shimmied down until we could jump across to a tree and then clambered down its long roots to the base of the cliff. Nearly there, we had to crawl in among huge boulders that had broken away from the rock wall thousands of years ago.

Once we were past the boulders, which brilliantly sealed the entrance to the secret pool from the outside world, we had a clear view of the incredible forty-metre pool that lay 200 metres below us and was surrounded by towering 200-metre-high cliffs. We dangled our feet into the void below and threw rocks into the abyss, listening to the falling silence for ages before they finally made a faint plop into the water so far below us. From where we sat, we could see the floodplains stretching out as far as the eye could see. The huge cliffs of the escarpment wall peeled away to the left and the right. There wasn't another human being in sight. We were on top of the world.

Lewis and Ama agreed it was the most epic place they had ever been. The fact that we'd to search it out ourselves, risking life and limb and crawling through a rock barricade to get there, made it so much more special. I no longer felt the effects of my hangover.

This place took my breath away. Going there is one of my most cherished memories of Kakadu.

Another day, as I pulled into the resort after a long ride, I saw my mate, Tyrone, one of the young handsome pilots – all the female staff were falling over themselves for him. We sat and had a beer for a while, and then he said: "Man, I wish I had a motorbike. It sounds like so much fun!"

That was an invitation I couldn't pass up! "Grab my other helmet, mate, and let's go!"

I took him out to an area not more than twenty minutes from where we were, across the dusty floodplains and through a shallow river. We came across the edge of a large billabong and found a huge herd of wild horses grazing in the grass opposite us. He was ecstatic!

"You can ride a bike, can't you?" I asked him.

"Yeah."

"Okay, sweet. I'll wait here. Take it slow and go and sit with them – it's pretty cool."

Tyrone was a good lad. He was still only twenty-four at the time but knew what he wanted in life. He would get up at 5 a.m. and work out in the gym for hours before starting his pre-flight checks. He was working for KakAir in order to get his flight hours up for his dream job as an air force pilot. Even though he was a big boy with a baby face, I could see he had it in him. He was driven, hardworking, dedicated. I had a feeling he was going to do great things in the future.

He came back from his stint on my bike, glowing.

"This is what I do when I get on my bike, my man," I grinned. "Do you now understand why I'm always on it?"

Tyrone and I did our pre-enlistment fitness testing together in Darwin towards the end of the season. I had reapplied for the army when I'd arrived in Darwin months earlier. At the time I still didn't know what I wanted to do with my life, so it was something, some kind of direction.

We were the last two standing on our testing day, and pushed through the sit-ups together side by side. I told Tyrone about my time in the Navy and the dive school, and how I had been just like him; in my case, wanting nothing more in the world than to be a clearance diver and a Special Forces soldier. He was so pumped for me – that I was going to chase that dream again, and we would be going into the service together.

I was given a recommendation to move forward with my application, which meant I was waiting on an enlistment date, and then I would be back into basic training with the young blokes. But something about that didn't feel right, and one night, weeks later, when we were having beers together, I told him that I'd been thinking about it and had decided not to go back into the service.

"What! How come?"

"I feel like that dream was taken from me when I was a young bloke, and because of that, I've always held onto it. But now I'm thirty-five. I have a whole lifetime of experience, and I feel that going back into the infantry will be fifty steps back for me. I have so much more to offer the world than catching bullets, and as much as I would love the camaraderie in the army, I know I can do bigger things with my life and my talent elsewhere. I needed to chase this dream again so I could let it go myself. I can see that now."

"When you put it like that, it makes sense. It doesn't matter where you go, you'll be sick at anything you go for, hey."

Tyrone was a good lad.

It wasn't always smooth sailing, though. I learnt to tune into my instincts. One day after work I suited up, but I just didn't feel right. Something was amiss. I kept going but when I got to the turn-off onto the floodplains, I stopped and sat with this uneasy feeling. I decided to turn back and go and watch the sunset somewhere else. I turned down another road and was pulling away in third gear when, there in front of me, was a huge bull buffalo standing in the middle of the road. I locked my brakes up and put the bike into a 180-degree turn. I had come within ten metres of the huge animal. I pulled away and, when I got some space between us, I stopped to see what he would do. The bull started running towards me, so I dropped the clutch and got out of there. I knew something hadn't been right. It pays to listen to your intuition.

But that first encounter with the buffalo didn't deter me from going out onto the floodplains; on the contrary, it made me even more excited to get out there and see more of them. I knew that going out to actively search for wild buffalo was dangerous, so I made sure I did everything I could to ensure my safety.

I had spent my whole life waiting around for something bad to happen, not pursuing my dreams because of the possibility that something, such as my wife leaving me, might happen – and look how that ended for me! No, there was no more room for holding back on hypotheticals in my life anymore. Bad shit happens all the time. I just had to get on with planning for the worst but living for the best.

I learnt that buffalo and pigs would run into the bush if they heard my bike coming. I realized this because, on more than one occasion, I came through the bush and into a cloud of dust. Buffalo have a very distinct smell, and I knew they had been there just before I'd come into sight. I started putting through the bush in second gear, looking through the scrub beyond the track. Buffalo can be twenty metres in front of you but almost invisible. Because of this, I was always totally amped up when I was on the hunt. But it wasn't the buffalo I was actually hunting; it was that feeling I got, the euphoria when I overcame something, when I conquered the beast, when something went wrong and I fixed it, when I was stuck in a bog and saved myself, when I was lost in a gorge and I made it out. There was always a moment of terror, and beating it was just an incredible feeling. I was hunting fear itself.

In a situation like this with the buffalo, I would park with a tree on my left and the bike acting as a shield on my right. That way, if it did go pear-shaped and a buffalo did charge out of the bush, I had an exit strategy. I might be in a tree, but at least I wouldn't be on the deck with an angry bull.

One day I went through this whole routine. I knew there were buffalo in the area; I had seen their tracks in the dust and could just feel them. I parked my bike, dismounted and crouched in the tall grass like a statue. My body was charged like a jack-in-the-box, ready to jump into the closest tree at the first sound of crashing undergrowth. I tuned in, scanned the bush in every direction, felt the adrenalin surge through my veins. I took a deep breath. I could feel the soft breeze on my face, smell the dust around me. Magpie geese squawked in flight over a nearby billabong. The dry brittle grass brushed the back of my hand.

After a few minutes, I felt confident that I hadn't been compromised. I stalked like a leopard to the edge of the tree line. Looking out onto the open ground, I saw that I had about 100 metres to cross before I hit the trees again. I ran across the open ground with the fear of being hunted threatening to buckle my legs and make me retreat. The sweat was pouring from my brow. I was still nearly 150 metres from my bike, cut off from the false safety it offered. I stalked through the trees to the edge of a huge billabong. There, less than 50 metres away, was a mob of about nine to twelve buffalo: a family group of bulls and calves just going about their business in the shallow waters. It was a beautiful moment. They stood close together, the smaller ones away from the deep water. They flicked their giant horned heads from side to side while small white egrets found perches on their giant backsides.

It was late in the afternoon. The sun was low on the horizon. The birds and wildlife of Kakadu were out in abundance, and I was there on the floodplain with them, at one with the land. I was in awe. This was just magic. How could I ever go back to the 'civilised' world and explain this to people? It was a moment I will never forget.

Toward the end of the season, the energy of the resort changed. Fewer tourists arrived and the staff started to get fewer and fewer shifts. Some staff left and continued on their adventures. I'd always known that this journey would eventually come to an end, and I didn't want to be the last man standing, so to speak, but seeing some of my mates leave hurt. What can I say? It was such a unique place to live and work. I'd become attached to the people.

Ama was one of the first to leave. I suddenly felt like my little Gypsy Lane oasis was an island, and I was all alone again. I sulked through that week and, as soon as I got a day off, decided to go for a ride to clear my head.

I shot off from the resort around 11 a.m. and headed straight for the floodplains again. Across the South Alligator River again. Through the sandy riverbeds again. Past some wild horses and flocks of exotic birds again. Around the swampy billabongs and through a city of giant termite mounds again. I had explored this area a few times before. I was confident I knew the lay of the land. Out there, there were no defined tracks; just wheel marks left by the few local Indigenous hunting game, or my own bike tracks from journeys past.

I came through a sandy riverbed a little too fast; the track veered suddenly to the left and I dropped my hips into the front of the tank, simultaneously kicking my left leg forward in the hope of bringing the bike around. It was too little, too late. The bike started the turn, but the back wheel grabbed an edge and flipped the bike forward. I went sprawling out of the saddle and landed forward of my bike on my chest with a faceful of sand.

It happened so quickly. It had nearly been a bad one. I sprang to my knees, closed my eyes, and took three deep breaths, scanning my body for pain or discomfort, and let the adrenalin settle down. I had done this before; I knew the drill.

I found some shade and took a muesli bar from my pack. I was down today. The adventure was over; it was coming to an end. I was sad with the realisation. I was sulking like a spoilt child.

The sun was beating down hot; it must have been about two in the afternoon. I decided to press on and head north, knowing that eventually I would cross the bitumen, refuel and head home.

The track eventually came to a murky billabong that was too deep to cross. The vines and pandanus plants were thick either side; after a quick inspection, I decided that it was too dangerous to attempt. I had seen more than enough crocodiles by then; I had developed a very healthy respect for the prehistoric reptiles, especially after seeing one try and take down a buffalo. I got anxious just standing near the water, let alone crossing water I couldn't see through.

But my fuel was low. I didn't have enough to get back to the resort if I backtracked. Forward was the only option.

I spent the next hour exploring up and down the banks, looking for a bottleneck. Once I was satisfied, I spent the forty-five minutes after that cutting a tunnel into the jungle with my hatchet that would be big enough for me to push my bike through. It was heavy work; I was drenched in sweat by the time I got back on my bike. I gunned the motor and cleared the murky waters with my first attempt, riding up the far bank through the exit I had cleared and back to the main sandy track. I mentally fist-pumped the air.

Suddenly I was back up again, and the sulking schoolboy was left behind in the billabong. I refuelled my bike approximately fifty km up the track. Now I had a decision to make: head back towards home, or north to the head of the West Alligator River?

The day was getting late, and the track up had only just dried out from the receding floodwaters. It was still very soft and untouched and I still had over 120 km to ride to get there. *Stuff it*, I thought, *what could possibly go wrong?* (Yeah, I know...)

The track up to the head, I had heard, was the worst in Kakadu. Whoever had told me that had not been lying. The bush changed half a dozen times, from vast open plains to grassy wooded lowland savannas. At one point I crossed a flood plain that was so vast that from the middle I couldn't see its borders in any direction. I would learn later that it was the biggest plain in all of Kakadu. It was like standing on a giant moonscape. I made sure to get a 360-degree shot with my helmet-mounted GoPro.

I kept pushing north. Dingoes and wallabies ran into the bush ahead of me. The track turned onto small rocky outcrops, and large, thick tree roots crisscrossed my path, forcing me to lift the front wheel to pass over them as smoothly as possible.

I finally rode out to the head of the river – and met John, Dawn, Anne and Lindsay from Victoria. They were the only other travellers out there, and the looks on their faces were priceless when I rolled into their camp.

"What the hell are you doing out here? Are you all alone? Where the hell did you come from? Do you have fuel, water, food? You're crazy!"

The achievement of getting out there in one piece, of having an epic day on the bike, and of seeing their reactions gave me another boost of energy. I was grinning like an idiot as I told them all about my adventures so far.

We took a few photos and spoke for a while. They were really nice people.

"You have absolutely made our day, Benji! Thank you so much for stopping in, but it's getting late. Please, stay the night. It's too dangerous to ride back anywhere now."

It was tempting to take them up on their offer but I had told the pilots I'd be back that night. I had no reception and couldn't make contact. I needed to get back to stop them from worrying and sending a search party. I knew Tyrone would be all over it, and I had planned to go to Darwin with him at 6 a.m. the next day. They wouldn't let me go without eating and drinking, so I quickly piled some food into my face, refilled my water bladder, and was back off into the bush.

The sun was getting dangerously low in the sky. I knew it was bad news to be out at dusk: all the animals come out to play then. But I was feeling sharp and I knew the track now. *If I can just get back to the bitumen before I lose the last of the light, it should be fine.* I tore through the bush as fast as I could, animals running into the bush away from me. I dared not take my eyes off the track as the trees and rocks flashed past in a blur.

The tree line broke and I found myself back out on the enormous flood plain I had stopped to appreciate on the way in. Only this time I had no time to stop and admire it. The sun was kissing the horizon over my right shoulder, so I twisted the throttle wide open. I was racing the sunset.

That was a once-in-a-lifetime moment. The sun was a huge orange orb on the western horizon. It slid deeper underneath as I urged my bike to go ever faster. The wind was roaring over me as my bike glided across the open plains. It was a magic feeling. In that moment, I was completely free, wild, *alive*. I was indestructible. WOOOOOOOOOOHOOOOOOOOOOOO! I howled into my helmet like a man reborn, free from the pain of self-loathing. The dark shadows of fear had all but dissolved from the deepest recesses of my self-esteem, and in their place had returned my self-worth, my belief, and my worthiness to call myself a man. I had proven the nay-sayers wrong! I laughed wildly into my helmet as I watched that beautiful sunset from the corner of my eye.

Then I was back in the trees. The wheels bounced across the ruts and kicked up a storm of dust behind me. I was up on the pegs; my body was one with the bike. My legs and arms absorbed the punishment the ground threw up at me and my bike glided over the sand and rock and through the trees effortlessly. At one point, a bat flew into my visor, snapping my neck backwards with the force of a stiff jab. (I knew it was a bat, because the next day I found it wedged under my helmet peak.) I laughed like a mad man and kept the bike roaring along.

Eventually I got to the roadhouse where I had originally refuelled. By then it was dark. There were no lights on; the place had become a ghost town. I sat by the bowsers, suddenly exhausted. I checked my fuel. I figured if I just putted along, I would come close to getting back, and if I didn't make it, then, worst case, I would have to hide my bike and walk the last 10-20 km home or just sleep in the bush. I liked those odds. I called ahead to give Tyrone my new SAR (Search and Rescue) time and putted off slowly into the night.

It took me over two hours to travel the last hundred kilometres. I felt that at any moment I was going to run my little bike dry. But I didn't want to stop. I just couldn't.

At one point, I came upon a big bull buffalo standing in the middle of the bitumen. By then I had seen so many buffalo in the park and I was just so tired that I felt I had no choice but to press slowly forward. As I putted ever closer towards him, he just looked over his shoulder at me with mild amusement. I passed within five metres of him on his rear side. I couldn't help but wave at him, say hi, and carry on. He didn't even blink, and I just kept putting along.

It was nearly midnight by the time I got back into the resort. I slowly made my way into the campgrounds and towards my van, my sanctuary. I was less than 30 metres from it when the bike stalled, starved of fuel. I was going so slowly, and it happened so suddenly, that it took me by surprise. I was exhausted by then, my legs so numb that I didn't even have the time to put them down. I collapsed in a heap with my bike and lay in the dirt, looking up at the stars. I had made it. I was home. I was alive!

When I had the energy to move, I peeled my helmet off, tossed it aside, and smiled to myself deliriously. *Good work, Brundin. Winning!*

Ever since I was a kid, when things went right in my life, or I pulled off an arsey shot, I would always laugh out loud and exclaim, "Winning!" to anyone who was in earshot. It felt like it had been so long since I'd made that victory cry, but now I was back on the winning side of life.

I had just ridden over 440 km across the floodplains of Kakadu. There was no more room for doubt. After that day, I knew I could ride to Cape York.

The energy of the resort continued to wind down. Someone was leaving almost daily. The food and beverage staff seemed to have more and more days off, which meant more and more staff lounging by the rec room pool. The tour guides were ready to kill one another: they were sick with the effort of fake smiling and telling old jokes, and they were over incompetent tourists. I knew it was time to move on but I felt such an attachment to the place. The idea of uprooting and starting again was hard to accept.

On my last day in Kakadu, I had planned to hike out to a huge waterfall I'd heard stories about. I rode my bike deep into the escarpment area and hiked from there into an enormous gorge. By this time I was so accustomed to venturing into the wild places alone that I felt confident of my ability to find my way back.

But perhaps this time I had spoken too soon... I crossed the waterways a dozen times, hiked up into the Stone Country and back down along foothills looking for those waterfalls. I flew my drone up the valley for two kilometres but there was still no sign of the falls I was seeking. I hiked for another two kilometres and did it again. For the better part of the day I was averaging three kilometres an hour but finally I had to admit defeat. I had run out of time to keep on adventuring in Kakadu.

I sat on a rock looking out over the valley below me, and instead of feeling upset I savored the moment. *Look at all you've achieved, Brundin. You have owned it out here, mate. There will be times again to chase these adventures. But right now your mates are waiting for you. Go have a drink with them, you dickhead!*

I raced back to the resort and arrived just in time for the going-away drinks that had been arranged.

It was a special night for me in Kakadu. I put on my best shirt and couldn't get the smile off my face. Even the Chinese girls came to share a drink and wish me a fond farewell. Their English was not the best, but they all gave me a hug and told me, "Benji, you are good man, always happy. You deserve a happy woman, happiness for your future. You are good man." The indigenous lads came up and we shared a smoke together. Some of the managers came to have a drink, which was unheard of. Mix with the staff? The pilots drove down from Jabiru and Jacob took a heap of photos for me. Lewis put me on the spot and got me up to make a speech, so I just blurted out the first thing that came to mind.

"Guys, thank you all so much for having a drink with me tonight. This has been a place of immense healing for me. It is absolutely incredible, and you guys have made it so. Here's to all of you. To great people, great adventures. Cheers!"

I'd packed up Gypsy Lane and had brought my van up to the rec room just for fun. At one point, we had the back overflowing with people. It was a real laugh.

I could see the respect I had earned through my adventures in the eyes of all the people I had come to know and love. I was quite emotional throughout the night.

Lusy came up to me at one point and thanked me for taking her out on what she described as her 'greatest adventure in Australia'. We had hiked into a secret oasis together, deep in the Stone Country, just weeks before.

Kasun hugged me and said, "Benji, my friend, when we think of you, we will always think of adventure. You're crazy, man. Come and visit me in Sri Lanka. You are welcome there always."

And even Steven, the gay Kiwi from the office, laughed with me. "Benji, what would season 2018 have been without Gypsy Lane? There are families in Australia that will never forget that place, and neither will we."

The next day I couldn't say any more goodbyes. I had to just leave. I was choked up as I pulled out of the resort. It had been such an epic journey for me: Kakadu had healed the deepest of wounds. But, like the seasons, it was a time for change. Soon the rains would come and drown the dusty plains. The tracks of adventure I had carved into the landscape would be washed away and the colourful blooms of a new season would spread across the land. This adventure had run its course, and I knew it. It was time for new journeys to begin.

My brothers were in Far North Queensland and I was looking forward to seeing them and catching up on all I had missed. The pages of life were turning. Another adventure was lying in wait, just around the corner.

Epic Kakadu: *https://www.youtube.com/watch?v=7rrT7SoC-Ec_*
Kakadu from the air: *https://www.youtube.com/watch?v=OYYXwZ3t0zk*
Creb Track on motorbikes:
https://www.youtube.com/watch?v=WdSooN5r2Xc&t=121s

BB – KEY #5: BUILD BELIEF IN YOURSELF BY TAKING ACTION

Once you have a plan and at least one person who supports you, you must begin to take action. The universe won't believe you are committed until you demonstrate it, but once you do... be ready! Doors will start to open for you and opportunities will fall into your lap.

Remember how all the doors closed for me when I was on the wrong track, and opened once I was on the right track? This will happen for you too!

That doesn't mean it will suddenly all be easy. There will be plenty of challenges along the way as well. I went through many periods of uncertainty during my travels but I just kept moving forward. Inertia is deadly; if you're in motion, you can always change direction. This is why it's so important to keep taking achievable action steps. You might be quaking in your shoes but taking action 'as if' you can do it will do wonders for your confidence, especially if yours is a 'crazy' goal.

If you're worried about something or you've hit a roadblock, ask yourself practical questions to put yourself in the right frame of mind for problem solving. *How can I fix this? Where can I get water? Who can I call for help?* The right language and creative questions will keep your mind in problem-solving mode and propel you forward. Maybe you need some training or education to feel confident enough to get started. Maybe you need some equipment. Maybe you need to find out how other people have tackled similar projects. Those things will do wonders for your confidence.

When you begin asking questions like this, your mind will become creative and start to present possibilities, but when you say things like, 'I can't do that' or 'it's too expensive', your brain will shut down those possibilities. Our brain always agrees with us and works to prove us right.

Practise now by identifying problems you face and asking yourself some useful questions. It doesn't matter if you don't have all the answers yet; you just need to start.

Here are a few questions to get you thinking:

What is in the way of me achieving my goal?

What am I afraid of?

What is holding me back?

What am I going to do about it?

Who can help me?

What do I need?

Where do I start?

Part of the escarpment wall, Kakadu

Captain Tyrone (Topgun) and I

Tyrone on the floodplains after chasing wild horses

Crocodile, Kakadu

Buffalo on the floodplains

Lewis the photographer and Ama the model, top of Kakadu

Lewis, Ama and Matt, good times on Gypsy Lane

Epic shots from Lewis (cheers, mate!)

Sunset over the floodplains, Kakadu

Happy days in the wild places

Last night in Kakadu, van fully loaded

Fighting fires on the airfield, Kakadu

NORTHERN POINT

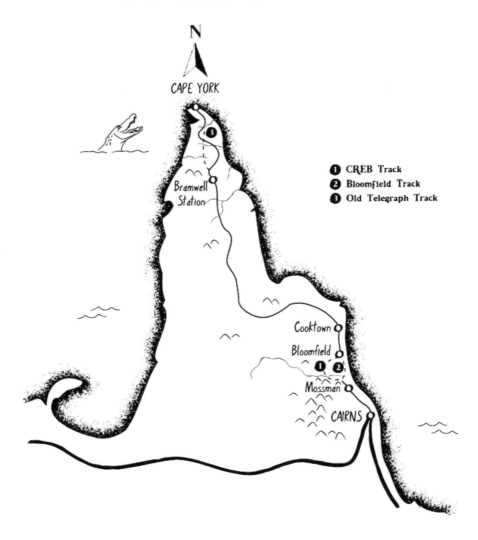

1 CREB Track
2 Bloomfield Track
3 Old Telegraph Track

Chapter 7
NORTH POINT, CAPE YORK

Dare greatly

- Brené Brown

I spent the next three days driving across the Territory and Queensland, racing to get to Cairns to catch up with my brothers and the rest of my family. There was a car rally event on in town and my brother Jarrod was the only person insane enough to be navigator for our crazy driver friend, Mick. Together they made a great team who would go on to win the Targa Rally Championship later in the year. They were at the top of their game, and it was great to be with them and catch up on the last six months.

I stayed with my sister and got to spend some quality time with my nephews who I hadn't seen in years. They were excited to hang out with their Uncle Benji and help me get my trip organised.

Driving into Cairns was like driving into a giant adventure playground. Cairns is located in Far North Queensland and is the most populated city north of Brisbane. It's also a popular staging ground for trips to the Great Barrier Reef, the Cape York Peninsula and the surrounding Atherton Tablelands. Tourism is a booming industry and the place just screams adventure.

The city itself has been built over lowland mangrove swamps and sand ridges. In the wet season, roads and sugarcane fields can flood and become impassable. Through the dry season, however, the climate remains warm and inviting. The town itself is surrounded by towering mountain ranges thick with dense, impenetrable rainforest. Driving in, the sight of the mountain ranges made me nervous. To get to Cape York, I would have to ride through them. I had never ridden in mountains before, and these ones were massive: steep and uninviting.

It took me just over a week to prep my bike and my gear, watch every bit of YouTube there was about the northern tip, and gather as much knowledge as I could from the local motorbike dealers.

From Cairns, I would have to ride out through the mountains and then almost a thousand kilometres through some of the most isolated country in Australia. Cape York is still regarded as one of the last great odysseys in Australia. The bush is wild, the rivers deep and full of crocodiles. As I watched endless videos of broken cars and men, four at a time, carrying their motorbikes across raging rivers, my heart sank. I felt real fear sit like a stone in my stomach. That familiar voice piped up.

Come back another day to do this, Benji. You won't get through the mountains on your own. Be smart; you have nothing to prove. You can't ride all the way there by yourself. You'll never get there – look at those rivers. You can't do it!

I met a few local guys who had done the trip to the Cape a dozen times, and peppered them with questions. "How many rivers are there? How deep are they? How many crocs have you seen? Has anyone ever not made it? Would you do it solo on a bike?"

"Too many to count."

"Deep enough to drown a truck."

"Lost count."

"All the time."

"No way, not a chance!" they all said. "You won't get through. You can go all the way up on the Peninsula Development Road (PDR) but that's cheating. You have to do the Old Telegraph Track for the last bit. Unless you do the OTT, it doesn't count."

I'd felt afraid at the sight of those churning rivers; now, the locals' confirmation of the danger of doing this trip on my own locked that fear in. And on top of that, there was the ego trip: I would have to do the route they considered the most dangerous or my success wouldn't even count.

I had been bullied as a young teenager, told that no matter what I did it was never good enough. There was still a little piece of me that just didn't want to give those old bullies any ammo to throw back at me. No, even if the locals hadn't said it, it was the OTT all the way. There was no middle ground.

My sister Tara, the wild child, said: 'You'll do it, Benji. I certainly wouldn't do it, but I believe in you. You'll get there.' Her endorsement meant a lot to me.

Before leaving Kakadu, Tyrone had given me a parting gift, a book called *Extreme Ownership.* The authors had been Navy Seals, and their ethos on life really struck a chord with me. They talked about ownership, about not passing blame, about taking full control of your life and your circumstances.

This was my extreme ownership moment. There was no one telling me to ride the Cape but me and my ego. If it went wrong up there, it was all on me. I needed to own everything.

I was a thirty-five-year-old living in a van because of choices I had made.

If I had a bad 'off' out there, it would be because I was going too fast.

If I lost my bike in a river, it would be because I hadn't taken absolutely every precaution I could to get through safely.

I was kicked out of the police, not because they were disorganised and politically corrupt, but because I had wanted to write books and inspire people.

My marriage ended because I was too self-absorbed to see our problems.

My marriage ended because I was too self-absorbed to see our problems…

My marriage ended because *I* was too self-absorbed to see our problems.

Sometimes, ownership sucked.

Before I left I wrote out my trusted fear formula and went over my whole bike. I made sure I had all the tools necessary to take the rear end apart and fix anything I thought could go wrong. I knew the rivers would be challenging, so I planned to take the rear swing arm out and walk the bike across in pieces if I needed to. It would be hard going, but I figured I could take the seat, battery and as much weight as I could out of the frame and take it across on my shoulder.

Fifteen years of roof tiling had made my back and shoulders as strong as an ox. I knew this wouldn't be too much of an issue. In case it did prove to be too difficult, I packed an additional length of strap so I could sling the frame under one shoulder like a gym bag. I also thought that I might be able to tie my inflated spare tubes to the frame and float it across.

I knew I had to pack light so I made sure my kit, drone and tools could fit in one racing bag, which I strapped to the back of my bike. Everything needed to be in one bag, because I knew I would be unstrapping it often to walk it across the rivers before I brought the bike across.

I had nearly come off once before in Kakadu when I'd hit a sandy washout and the whole bike had nearly dug in. Because of this, I made a very strict rule: if I was on the dirt, I was on the pegs. That way, complacency couldn't set in on longer stretches of track. I also set the rule of walking the exact line I was going to take on every water crossing I came across; that way I could feel every rock and hole in the river bed before I hit it with my tyres. Non-negotiable!

I ensured my first aid kit was clean and ready for use, my texta was in perfect working order, my tools accounted for, my bike in top condition, my spare air filters oiled and sealed in their snap-lock bags, my knives sharp, and my maps dry and memorised. (I took maps because I didn't have enough ports to charge my camera gear as well as a GPS, and I didn't trust a GPS signal out there).

I was ready.

Before leaving, I wrote an expedition brief to myself, stating the objective of the trip: to safely get to the northernmost point of the mainland via the entire OTT and back again. I wrote down all the risks I could think of and how I could reduce them. I wrote a list of every possible worst-case scenario and what I could implement to overcome it.

At the end of my brief, I wrote a note to myself. *Benji, it is good to be nervous. It means you're not cocky. This is going to be tough, but you can do it! Do all your checks like you normally do. Take your time and remember all you have learnt. You can do this. Feel the fear – and do it anyway!*

On 12 September 2018 I left Cairns, feeling very out of place as I putted around the roundabout and through the traffic lights in all my gear. I headed out to Port Douglas and Mossman and then onto the Creb Track. The Creb Track is an eighty-kilometre muddy track that cuts straight through the thick mountain ranges; the hill climbs are long and steep, the rivers wide.

After a few offs, and one where I flipped the bike, I had to put my ego aside. I had no experience in the mountains. I wasn't a good rider. The objective was to get to the tip alive, so I decided to go back down the mountain and take the less arduous Bloomfield Track instead – still steep, but wider and better maintained. If I were to have any chance of still being alive to tackle the notorious OTT (Old Telegraph Track) for the final stretch, I needed to pace myself. By the time I got back to Cape Tribulation, it was time for a beer and an early night.

Day Two saw me come out of the mountains into dusty bushland. The dirt roads were covered in loose stones. I lost count of the river crossings by the third day. I met another solo rider at an isolated roadhouse, and he directed me to take a 'road less travelled' through Aboriginal land.

On Day Three I passed a total of six cars, all heading south. I had camped the previous two nights, so I thought the ten dollars the Coen pub was charging for a campsite and hot shower was good value. I met a lovely girl there and she invited me to stay at hers and cooked me breakfast. You just have to love country hospitality.

By Day Four, the roads deteriorated even further and were the worst I had ridden in Australia. I had done close to 800 km on the pegs by then, so my legs were feeling it. The washouts were long, sandy and dangerous. The rocks in the middle of the road were the size of tennis balls – even soccer balls at times. There were burnt-out shells of cars in both directions. Some had once been top-of-the-range four-wheel drives. I can't imagine how devastated someone would have been to come all this way, only to destroy their car before even getting to the 'hard part'.

Though it was a short day on the bike, I was grateful for another warm bed at Bramwell Station. There I met another convoy of travellers who would also be heading north up the track, so I had dinner with them. While we ate and talked about the track conditions we were about to venture into, the station host gave us a rundown of the station, hammering home how isolated we were.

"An ambulance from Weipa is a minimum of three hours away. The Royal Flying Doctor service is a one-hour flight – that is, if there's a pilot available. If. And that's just to get to Bramwell. So if you do have an accident out there, you could be hours, even days, from help. Please keep that in mind. The track conditions are the worst they have ever been. Did anyone see the parked four-by-fours at the start? They aren't parked, they're broken, waiting for tow."

The next day I woke early and got myself a big brekkie. I was about to ride my bike onto the Old Telegraph Track. One of the most iconic tracks in Australia, it is over a hundred kilometres long, the sand is deep, the rivers deeper – and my legs were already shot. I was as nervous as I had ever been in my life.

That track was absolutely epic. Trees and scrub crowded the track on either side, threatening to grab my kit bag and pull me into the bush. I didn't wear gloves because it was over 30 degrees, so the back of my left hand was soon covered in cuts. I was totally immersed in the experience of being there.

Over the next two days, every time I arrived at a river crossing I'd do a quick scan for crocs and then dive into it in full kit, desperate to cool down. I drank the water straight from the river; it was deliciously cool and I gulped it down like sweet mango juice on a hot day.

Each crossing was different, so I dared not take the chance of not walking them first. Some rivers had hard rocky bottoms, but these were the most dangerous because there were deep holes in the rocks. If you didn't pick your lines well and put your front wheel into one of the holes, it was all over. Another looked so clear and inviting with a nice pebbly bottom, but when I walked through it, the water came up to the middle of my leg. I had to ride my bike down the river, hugging the left bank, before I could cross at a shallow point, and then hug the bank back up to the track on the right-hand side.

I met other travellers on the journey but preferred to go at it alone. One group saw me humping my bag across a river and offered to take it; I kindly declined, explaining that I just wanted to get it done myself.

"I totally get that, man. Good luck, bro. You're f#@king crazy!"

"I know! Ha-ha," and I waved back at them as I tore off into the bush.

I stopped in at Fruit Bat Falls. The place was deserted… apart from a carload of young nurses who had driven up from Weipa for a few days. So poor me had to wash the dust off and make new friends.

I met three guys from Brisbane at the notorious Gunshot Creek crossing: Jarod, Callum and Mick. They were on a boys' trip of a lifetime, and had five weeks to explore the whole Cape. Cal held my GoPro while I dropped into the steep entry point. He had a KTM bike back home, and a lot of experience. When I told him I'd never ridden down anything that steep before, he thought I was kidding.

"I've only been riding for six months," I explained.

He offered some advice on the crossing.

They loved that I was out there on a $3000 dirt bike with a cheap saddlebag tied to the tank with a piece of Telstra rope.

"Mate, you are camping with us! We have all this beer that we're not allowed to take over the Jardine River, so you need to help us drink it!"

Those guys were awesome. Between them, they owned an auto-electrical and a boat-building business, so their trucks were decked out with the best of everything. They had ovens, icemakers, fridges, freezers, fans, subwoofers – the works! Jarod loved to cook. That night, in the middle of one of the most isolated and remote parts of the country, we ate a dinner of grain-fed Wagyu beef and a walnut salad drizzled with a fine honey glaze. I offered them all a glass of Captain Morgan rum, which I'd packed for such occasions, but they wouldn't have a bar of it.

The next morning, feeling slightly rusty, we ate free-range bacon and eggs for breakfast and brewed real coffee, complete with frothed milk. After another swim, we set off and I filmed them crossing rivers and tackling some harsh terrain as a way of saying thanks. But I pushed my luck too far and lost my drone in a tree. We spent nearly three hours looking for it. We started with a search area of about 200 metres by two before I yelled out in triumph, finally finding it less than two metres from where we had parked the cars.

It was a pretty harsh reminder for me, though. In all of that time, not one other car had passed. If I had an accident out here, help was a long way away.

After losing so much time searching for the drone, the day was getting on and I wanted to get the track finished. I said my goodbyes and pushed on alone.

I crossed more rivers and got lost a few times but pressed on. One group of travellers gave me some sound advice.

"Once you cross the next river, there's a track that will take you back onto the PDR. If you keep going up the OTT, you'll come to Logan's Ford. It's deep – too deep for a bike; another guy drowned his bike there yesterday. But if you do cross it, you won't get back across that way. After Logan's there are a few more crossings until the last at Nolan's Brook. That's the one that kills all the cars. It's too deep apparently, so we decided not to go on. Good luck, buddy."

When I got to Logan's Ford, they were totally right. The water was clear and deep through the middle, but there were swampy reeds up and downstream.

The hair rose on the back of my neck again as I waded in. It was soon over my belly button. My first aid kit, saturated long ago, was

BENJI BRUNDIN

completely submerged on my hip as I walked through, looking for a line. I unstrapped my kit bag for what felt like the hundredth time and walked it over. Then I waited for a car to arrive. After about twenty minutes, none had come past so it was up to me to go at it alone. It was getting late, so I didn't want to waste any more time. I decided to cross on the far right of the deep water and give it a go. This was what I signed up for, after all.

I rode into the water and up onto a muddied island in the middle. The bike stuck hard on a submerged tree root. I rocked it back and forth and splashed about for what felt like ages. I dared not look around for a giant crocodile. I finally got the bike unstuck and made it across in one go. I was totally ecstatic and couldn't keep myself from twisting the throttle and doing a big doughnut in the soft sand on the far side. I knew that if Jarod, Cal and Mick came past, they would see that I had made it this far. (They never did: after getting some sound advice, they too took the track back out to the PDR). Now I was past Logan's Ford. I was one hundred per cent committed; there was no turning back. The only way off the OTT was north, through Nolan's Brook, the deepest river on the Cape.

Not too much further up the track, I came across another deep crossing. I unstrapped my gear and humped it across again, and again, the water was up around my naval in the middle where countless four-wheel drives had dug the steep entry points out. I met another group there that I'd met the previous day at a different crossing. Graham, Tony and I walked up and down the banks looking for an entry point for the bike.

The crossing itself had about five different entry points. Almost all were vertical, dropping down about 1.2 metres into a deep sandy riverbed. In a four-wheel drive, the water would be up over the bonnet as you drove through. There simply weren't any entry points I could take my bike through.

But there was one spot where I could ride my bike along a narrow patch of bank to the water's edge. It was about half a metre wide there, with a drop into the water on one side and thick bush on the other. At the end, I could launch my bike off the drop-off and, if I could keep my momentum, clear the deep channel of water and land in the shallow water on the far side.

"This looks like your best option, mate."

The choice was simple: try the other crossings and definitely drown my bike, or try this and maybe drown my bike. At that point, I was feeling pretty confident. I had beaten everything the track had thrown at me so far. I wasn't just feeling confident; I was full of confidence.

I gave Graham my GoPro, ran back over to my bike, and started my approach. No helmet, hat backwards, I crept along the narrow bank and launched at the deep water. When the bike landed, the water splashed up over the handlebars but thankfully the momentum kept me pushing forward. Graham and his group were cheering and I had the biggest cheesy grin on my face. I didn't realize it at the time, but I had just jumped my bike across Nolan's Brook. (Later I discovered there was a log bridge for motorbikes to cross just a bit further up the river.)

Graham and his group headed out while I repacked my gear and checked over my bike yet again.

The track continued ever north. Huge cavernous erosions split the track at one point; then it would be rocky boulders and hard-pressed earth, then back to sandy savannah. At one point, I could see the smoke of a huge grass fire over my right shoulder. It was a long way off, so I didn't give it another moment's thought. The sandy track suddenly got very deep and kept pulling me into the bush. One of the straps holding my bag on came loose and got caught in my rear wheel; the strap snapped with a loud crack. I looked down and straightaway regretted the decision. Next thing I knew, I was sprawling in the bush.

I checked over my bike and saw that the strap had wedged in tight around the rear wheel hub and it was going to take some time to cut it loose with my Leatherman. While I worked, the wind swirled around me and the smoke of the grass fire came over in thick blankets. I was all alone, with a bushfire somewhere nearby. Those were a few nervous minutes for me as I worked frantically to get the strap loose.

I kept pushing hard through that section of track, which eventually came to a big loop. It took me a moment to realize that I had come to the end of the track.

I had arrived at the banks of the Jardine River. I couldn't go any further; I was totally spent, covered in cuts and bruises from head to toe. I had ridden over a thousand kilometres to get here, crossed countless rivers, had dozens of falls. I had worn the same riding gear for six days. My boots had been wet since day one and my feet were water-logged and tender. But I was totally alive. I stood on the banks and raised both arms in the air, elated. After all the rivers and the offs and the smoke of the fire, it was a very emotional moment.

Graham and the rest of his group were there; they had arrived just minutes before me. "Congratulations, mate, you've just completed the entire Old Telegraph Track."

I was shaking as I hugged them all. That last 10-15 km of the OTT is hardly ever used anymore but I hadn't wanted anyone telling me I'd skipped the hardest part; now that I'd ticked that box, I still had to backtrack to the main track and out onto the PDR so I could get to the tip the next day, and it was already late.

By the time I got to the Jardine Ferry Crossing, it was just on dusk. I quickly set my little tent up and crawled in. I was so spent, I didn't have the energy for a shower. I lay on my back and fell into a deep, satisfied sleep.

The next morning, I took the ferry over and rode the last 40 km or so up to Cape York. I ran into Jarod, Cal and Mick on the way and we stood on the tip of the Cape together, looking out over the small islands peppering the Torres Strait. It was a pretty awesome feeling to be gathered around the little sign, all cheering that we had conquered the Cape!

Back at the cars, I couldn't help myself and rode my bike up and down the deserted beaches, helmet off, the wind roaring into my face. I was invincible.

We eventually left and went our separate ways. I decided to spend one more night at the Punsand Bay camping grounds just to get a warm shower and a cold tap beer. I met the group of travellers I'd had dinner with at Bramwell Station, and we made sure we took a photo and had a few beers together. The next morning I rode back out to the tip again.

The walk to the tip takes you up and over a rocky peninsula. From the top you can see out in every direction. In the north, islands pepper the ocean all the way to Papua New Guinea. On the western edge of the peninsula palm trees and tropical jungles stop abruptly at the edge of pristine sandy beaches, while in the south and east, dense jungle spreads across the land. The beaches and jungles here are teeming with wildlife, snakes, crocodiles and wild pigs, to name a few. It's a wild, beautiful, savage place.

I sat on a rock by the sign and watched the currents of the Torres Straight roar past, taking turtles and seaweed with it. I spent an hour or so, uninterrupted, with my own thoughts.

I thought about all that had happened to me, and all that I'd been able to conquer and achieve. It had been an incredible journey. I promised myself that I would never forget, that I would share this journey with the world and immortalise my story in a book.

I knew I had done something special. The amount of support I had received from people back home every time I posted a new video to YouTube told me this. In the past I had let fear dictate the terms of my life. I had set great limitations on myself because of it. I now knew that I could overcome anything, that I had it in me to be and do anything I put my mind to. My self-worth and confidence had returned. It was now time to start the slow road home.

And I missed home. Although it would be almost another three months before I got back to Melbourne, I now knew where home was. My time away had allowed me to look back on my life and appreciate what it meant to have family. I might not have been born into my family, but Victor, Jenny and all my brothers and sisters had always been the ones I'd fallen back on. They had always been there for me, and always would be.

As I sat on the rock and looked at the seething water below, I thought about what I'd write in my book. I had learnt a lot about myself on the back of that bike. I also knew that if I applied all I'd learnt out here when I was back in the 'ordinary world', I could be happy and successful once again.

I am not a fearless person, and I know there are still many other areas of my life where I have yet to address fears, but one thing I did learn was this: on the other side of gut-crippling fear lies freedom, and when you face those fears you tap into that freedom, and the greatest adventures await you. That, I can promise.

Cape York odyssey: *https://www.youtube.com/watch?v=B53pIWBRUek*

BB – KEY #6: RESILIENCE.

This is the key to success in any endeavour. No person in the history of mankind has ever achieved greatness or success without buckets of resilience. Things are going to go wrong in life; this simple fact is unavoidable if you want to live a full life. Even people who don't want things to go wrong and spend their time avoiding conflict or hardship are going to experience rejections, breakdowns and pain. It is simply irrational to think that you can get through life without them.

So if hardship is inevitable, why not experience those setbacks working towards your best life, rather than just existing through life?

Do everything you can to build your levels of this essential ingredient. Get fit, read books, educate yourself, and just get out there and start living! Make bad choices, learn from them and keep pushing forward. You need rejection and disappointment in life in order to build resilience, and the only way to have those experiences is by living. And there's another reason: the sweet will never taste as good without a decent dose of the bitter.

How long has it been since you failed? Since you really had a crack at something? Since you risked embarrassment or disappointment? Is it time to tackle that secret goal or ask that person out?

Get up and out there and start getting rejected! The more often you are rejected, the stronger you will become and the better equipped you will be to deal with life's setbacks. Suck up the pain and develop a good amount of the internal wonder drug called Resilience. Guaranteed!

List the painful experiences you've had in the past that have started to build your reserves of the Resilience wonder drug. Anticipate what might go wrong in the future so you are armed and ready for it! (That's not negative thinking; it's being responsible and 'forward thinking'.)

Burnt-out cars on the PDR

TRAVERSE

N°09 · DECEMBER 2018 / JANUARY 2019

ALLEZ DU MAROC
The Price of a World Championship

WORLD RECORD ATTEMPT
A Young Bloke & His Ducati

WE ARE STRONG, WE ARE BEAUTIFUL
Women Riders World Relay

AN OLD MAN ...
AND HIS RIDE THROUGH THE STANS

THERE'S CROCS IN THERE
A FIRST ATTEMPT AT RIVER CROSSINGS

FROM RUSSIA WITH LOVE
A LASTING IMPACT FROM A WONDERFUL COUNTRY

"COVERED IN PISS & SPEW"
HOW BENJI BRUNDIN BECAME A MOTORCYCLE TRAVELLER

My story hits the front cover of a magazine

Standing on top of the world, Cape York, September 2018

Chapter 8
EAST POINT, FRASER ISLAND

I know he'd be a poor man if he never saw an eagle fly

- John Denver

After a few months in Cairns, living with my sister and hanging out with my nephews, it was time to start the journey back south. I had conquered the Cape, the hardest part, so it felt like the adventure was over. I drove the east coast like a spoilt schoolboy, impatient to get out of Noosa and its Beverley Hills footpaths. The whole place felt plastic to me.

I sulked in the bar at Airlie Beach and hardly noticed the beautiful backpackers walking around. To me, the whole east coast of Australia felt like one giant theme park.

By the time I got to Fraser Island I was in a real funk. I couldn't be bothered riding across the island and going on yet another adventure. It all just seemed like hard work by then. *Suck it up, Brundin! Jesus Christ, listen to yourself! Get on your bloody bike!*

Fraser Island is a natural anomaly. It is the largest sand island in the world, made by the tides from the south washing the sand up on the currents. It stretches north to south with an incredible 75-mile beach running almost its entire length on the eastern shores. It is home to over 74 different species of reptiles, 350 different species of birds and over 50 species of mammals. One in particular is the dingo. On Fraser Island there are hundreds of dingoes.

Its vegetation consists of dense tropical jungles, sand dunes and wooded bushland. It is the only place in the world where tall rainforests grow in sand. It has over 100 freshwater lakes and creeks. The aboriginal name for the island is K'gari, which translates as Paradise. They got it right: it is incredibly stunning and completely took me by surprise.

The mainland town of Hervey Bay, where the ferry is located, was overflowing with tourists when I drove in. Caravans blocked intersections, grey nomads proudly decked out in Hawaiian shirts, straw hats and bumbags walked without purpose in and out of the retail outlets. *F#@king tourists,* I thought as my van joined theirs in the convoy. I just wanted to get out of there as soon as I could.

I went to one of the many local resorts and asked the receptionist about the island and what to expect when I got there.

My plan was simple: take the ferry across to the west coast of the island. Ride my bike to the east coast and then up the hard, packed sand of the beach all the way to an old resort where I was assured I could get a bed. Then ride the rest of the way to the lighthouse the next day. Take the photo and return to the ferry. Easy. So easy, in fact, that I almost didn't go. *The place is just going to be packed with tourists. F#@king tourists. Why the hell would I want to go to a bloody theme park?*

I packed light, expecting a scenic ride through a well signposted tourist road to a cosy resort with a warm bed. In short, I left my camping gear and normal survival kit behind.

The ferry docked and I rode down the compressed gravel road into the thick rainforest, bum on seat, expecting more of the same.

Within 100 metres the track turned into deep rutted sand. I was taken completely by surprise and nearly lost my front wheel. I stood up on the pegs and brought all my weight to the rear, twisting the throttle on to bring the front end up and out of the sand. All of a sudden I was in it and fighting to stay upright as the track twisted and turned through the thick jungle vegetation. Giant prehistoric trees crowded the shoulders each side. There was no room for error. The sand sucked at my bike like the current of a raging flood. And the bike kicked and bucked below me, fighting like a rodeo bull. My torso moved with the bike, my legs compressed like giant springs to keep the balance centred. Above my shoulders, my head was steady, my gaze sharply focused in on the track, constantly scanning for the next line. It was awesome!

I nearly made contact with a few lone four-wheel-drives, all heading the other way and trying to maintain momentum. The sand on Fraser has lower clay content than desert sand, so it's looser, making it harder to gain traction. Parts of that island were by far the deepest sand I have ever ridden in.

I eventually made it out to the eastern coast and the famous 75 Mile Beach. I refuelled at the resort there and grabbed a bite to eat.

From there I headed north to the beach. The tide was out, which made riding absolutely exhilarating. I leant back and let my little bike stretch her legs. Creeks drained back into the receding surf and I splashed through with ease. And then the track would veer left and up and over a headland where the sand was brutally soft again.

At one point I was cruising peacefully along the hard, pressed sand at the water's edge when I saw that the track up ahead ventured back into the forest and there was a four-wheel drive bogged to the axles at the base of a dune. All its occupants were taking turns on the shovel between sips of beer.

I had to maintain my momentum so I just gunned it straight towards the dune. I was a passenger on my bike as it bounced across the heavily chewed-up beach. The wheels of countless four-wheel drives had carved deep ruts in the beach north to south. I was heading across them toward my dune and the bogged truck.

One of the occupants saw me coming and got the attention of the rest of the group. They all started to cheer me on and salute me with their beers as I passed within 10 metres of them. It must have been crazy to watch. The bike tore up the dune and as I crested the top I fist-pumped the air to acknowledge their support. *Hahahaha… Winning!!!*

By the time I was in the vicinity of my resort destination I was buggered. As I paid for my fuel, I spoke with the attendant.

"G'day mate. Where's the resort? I just want to get a room for the night."

"You won't get one here, mate. The resort was destroyed in a cyclone 25 years ago."

Turns out my info was bad.

"There's no point heading further north today: the tides are turning and soon the beach will be unpassable. Also, hardly anyone goes north from here; if you go that way, you're on your own. Your best bet will be to backtrack the 40-odd km to Cathedral on Fraser, but you best be quick. As I said, the tides are turning."

The ride back to the campground was just crazy. The tides were quickly coming up and so I was forced to ride at the top of the beach where it was extremely soft and chewed up. My bike only had factory gear ratios so it wasn't set up for sand this deep and I had to keep shifting between second and third gears as I tried to get on top of it.

My bike started overheating and green coolant began to spew out of it like arterial blood. I took a chance and tried to ride at the water's edge; only now, with the incoming tide, it was like soup. The front dug in and I went straight over the handlebars.

I picked my bike up as the waves came crashing over it. "F#@K!" I exclaimed and threw my helmet up the beach in frustration.

I was suddenly feeling very vulnerable. I had no water left. Over 20 km to get to the camp, no coolant in my radiator, no camping gear or food, and the tide was still rising.

If you get stuck out here, Brundin, the first thing we are going to do is carve a big bloody club to keep the dingoes at bay through the night.

The wild dingoes of Fraser Island had a reputation for being opportunistic. In 2019 a small boy was taken as he slept, and was bitten repeatedly around the back of his head and neck as the dingo tried to run off with him.

The ride back to camp after I'd come to grips with my predicament was intense! The small inlets I had splashed through in low tide were now like raging rivers. At one point I saw the eroded banks of a creek nearly four metres wide. I had to think quickly – I didn't dare slow down or I'd be sure to come off and then I'd be in real trouble as I still needed to cross the creek. All I could do was keep my momentum up and charge off the edge of the bank and into the water below. And trust that I'd power straight through.

For a moment my bike was like a submarine... And she popped her periscope out the other side and kept on motoring along. I laughed out loud again!

That night I spoilt myself with a small cabin, and as I shook the buckets of sand from my boots, riding gear and helmet, I started working out the plan I would need to travel the 200-odd km to get to the lighthouse and back to the ferry. I had been caught out because I had not shown the island the respect it deserved. I wouldn't let that happen again.

When are the tides low?

How much time will I have?

What food will I need?

Who can I contact if I don't return?

What will I do about the dingoes if I'm beached out there?

What I didn't realize at the time was that there was no little voice telling me it couldn't be done, it was too dangerous; for once, my 'pro' and 'con' voices were working together. There were no more self-imposed roadblocks holding me back.

The next day I got to the lighthouse, took the photo, and rode back to the ferry through a thunderstorm.

Although it was a relatively short adventure by comparison with the others, Fraser Island was nothing short of an odyssey that deserves as much respect as any of the compass points.

Fraser Island Adventures: *https://www.youtube.com/watch?v=26z9_E0ufUA*

BENJI'S KEYS TO 'MISSION SUCCESS'!

#1: A Goal: You need to start any venture with the end in mind, and that 'end' must *truly* matter to you. *What* you want to achieve needs to be clear in your mind's eye; don't worry yet about *how* you're going to achieve it. Expect to be both supported and challenged when you announce your goal.

#2: A Why: You need to have a clear understanding of *why* you are going to do this thing. Money is generally not a big enough motivator. It needs to be something bigger than you – for your family, to help others, for your health (whether physical, mental, emotional or spiritual).

#3: A Plan: The more detailed the plan, the better. It needs to incorporate every possible scenario and include contingency plans for overcoming challenges when things go wrong. With each step you take, the next step will become clearer. Visualisation helps immensely.

#4: A Team: You need to surround yourself with a team of people who share your vision – who believe in you and what you can achieve, and will keep you accountable.

#5: Build Belief By Taking Action: You develop belief by taking action on goals that are truly in line with what you want to do. If you don't yet really believe in yourself, just act as though you do and that you are capable of achieving your goal. Momentum is magical. When obstacles show up, keep the creative side of your brain engaged and working for you by asking practical questions.

#6: Resilience: When things go wrong, and they will, you need huge buckets of this. Set your focus back to your goal and why you are doing this thing and you will generate the resilience to get you through the hard times. Stay strong.

The northern lighthouse, Fraser Island.

The deep sand of Fraser Island

Chapter 9
THE DESERTS

Fate whispers to the warrior: 'You cannot withstand the storm.'
And the warrior whispers back: 'I am the storm.'
- Unknown

I arrived back in Melbourne in early December 2018. By Christmas, I was already climbing the proverbial walls. It turned out I just wasn't ready to come back yet. Without a new goal to focus my attention on, I was like a kelpie on a broken chain, with my mind constantly moving from one idea to the next, one project to another. My restlessness provoked quite a bit of anxiety and it wasn't long before I started to wear out not only myself, but also my friends and my family.

I knew I had more to prove, more to give, more to achieve. I started to look for additional adventures I could sink my teeth into. The Simpson Desert had been done to death, but what I found was that not many of the other deserts in Australia really get a mention – or not as far as motorbike crossings were concerned. I did my research and, by the start of the new year, I'd hatched a plan to cross all ten Australian deserts, solo and unsupported, on my little 250. To make sure I couldn't find a reason to back out, I announced my intention to be the first person to do so on social media. I even applied to Guinness World Records® to have this potential world record recognised.

And that was it. My hyperactive mind suddenly had a project to anchor onto. I had another adventure to immerse myself in. I could escape the normality of everyday life again! The goal was set; now I just needed a plan.

I rented a little bungalow close to my boxing gym where I could focus on being fit and stay in regular contact with my trainer and the other guys there. I got a job in construction to create some structure and balance in my life. And I started planning an adventure that would take me over thirty days to complete and see me riding across ten deserts and 6000 km of sand dunes, corrugated tracks and rocky outcrops.

Seventy per cent of the Australian continent is made up of desert, the majority of which is uninhabited. Only three per cent of the population lives in these regions. That makes Australia the driest inhabited continent in the world, right next to Antarctica. The deserts themselves cover an area of nearly 1,500,000 square km. If it went bad out there, no one was coming to save me.

When I thought about it all in one go, I got overwhelmed with the danger and fear. But I knew I could do it. If I applied everything I had learnt, I could get the job done. That was how I approached it – as a job. Not a holiday but an expedition, a mission or an odyssey. Without one hundred per cent commitment to and respect for the expedition, the consequences could be fatal. So even the words I used to describe this journey had to be aligned with the commitment needed to complete it.

I turned my little bungalow into an expedition room. Above my sink, I hung a huge map of Australia and carefully plotted my route. I studied every piece of footage I could get on YouTube and the internet about deserts. Interestingly, I couldn't find much information on the Australian central and western deserts. Not many people had done them on a motorbike.

I drew a big picture of the Wolfe Creek Crater and stuck it above my map. I drew myself standing on the rim with my motorbike next to me, knowing that this was the finish line. I visualised myself standing there every day.

I wrote down comprehensive stage notes for each kilometre of track I would traverse and committed to memory all the fuel stops, the distances between each, and how much fuel I would need to carry, as well as the Aboriginal communities I would need to send resupply packs to. I stuck these notes up around my room and made sure I knew them intimately. I had the name and distance for each stretch of track, the names of the police at each station I would come across as well as their phone numbers.

I took the steel tools out of my tool kit and replaced what I could with alloy to keep the weight down. I had my bike rebuilt from the ground up and had custom suspension installed front and back. Stel and his team at OnPoint Motorbikes got right on board and did hours of work for free.

'We all want to see you get through this thing, mate. It's insane!'

And when I announced on a motorbike riders' forum that I was doing the ride to raise money for The Black Dog Institute and mental health awareness, I was lucky enough to get into contact with Darren.

Darren was in his fifties. He'd worked hard his whole life and been smart with his money. He was also going through a divorce. He loved motorbikes and had spent time in most of Australia's deserts over the course of numerous trips. When we met, he was limping around with a knee brace on, the price you pay for going too quickly through the bush. Because he couldn't ride anymore, he was going slowly crazy in the confines of his broken home. He wanted to help me get the job done.

"We all know someone who is struggling with mental health, mate. You have a good heart. I want to see you get to the end of this thing alive!"

Darren was awesome. We would meet at his place and spend hours talking about my kit, weighing everything, throwing stuff away and repacking it all into my postie-bike saddlebags.

We even went away one weekend to Big Desert in Western Victoria (not actually a defined Australian desert) on a training ride where he limped to the top of a sand dune and watched me ride over it again and again and again, constantly yelling instructions to me.

"Squeeze your knees! Chin up, look forward! Elbows, elbows, elbows!" It was hilarious. It reminded me of something out of a movie – the old master and the apprentice.

There were so many people who helped me get it all together: David from Alenson Design helped with my logos, Shahn helped with all of my social media and website stuff. I had first aid kits and fuel bladders sponsored to me for the ride. But Darren was the real backbone of my team.

My family weren't as impressed, though. Jenny was rarely upset with me, but this time she made no attempt to hide her concern. "There is a very good reason no one has ever done it before, Benji. You understand that, don't you?"

Victor was blunt: "World champions break their bones every day, Benji. Who do you think you are? It can't be done!"

I knew they were worried. I understood that their concern came from a place of love. But they hadn't seen what I had done. They didn't know what I knew. They hadn't seen my expedition room. Their concern brought negativity to what I needed to focus on, and I could not afford to poison my mind with it. I needed to maintain my belief that I could get it done. I had to create distance from the people I loved.

Seven months went by in the blink of an eye. Before I knew it, I was in the small town of Marree in South Australia, about to enter my first desert. It was 10 July 2019, and I was petrified.

Even though I knew the first 500 km were going to be a relatively flat albeit corrugated road, I couldn't help but feel that familiar snake coil around in my stomach.

You've done the work, Benji. What's the worst thing that can happen?

The truth was actually the complete opposite. My bike had spent a month longer in the shop than I had hoped because we kept finding mechanical issues that needed to be fixed. That bike had had a pretty hard life, don't forget! I'd ridden it a total of two times since the rebuild, and was stiff and sore for days after just riding 120 km in training a few weeks earlier.

Now I had the Simpson Desert to take on – not just any desert, the largest parallel sand dune desert in the world, and I needed to cross over a thousand of those dunes to get to the other side.

I will never forget the first night I camped out in the Tirari desert. I lay in my sleeping bag, staring at the roof, thinking over and over again, *What the hell do you think you're doing, Brundin? It's still not too late to turn around. Sabotage the bike or do something. No one will think less of you.*

A few days later I was standing in the Simpson thinking the exact same thing.

I had arrived at the base of Big Red, the first dune from the eastern end of the desert and certainly the biggest. I'd planned to camp at its base to get an early start into the desert the next day. It was getting late in the day but I wanted to do some quick exploring!

I unpacked all my saddlebags and joined a few other four-wheel drives in attempting to summit the unforgiving mountain of sand. The heavyset cars would get a run-up from hundreds of metres back on the clay pan and send huge roosters of sand into the sky as the big diesel engines worked hard to get up. I left my gear out on the pan and hit the dune fast in third gear. Halfway up the bike started to bog down and I quickly snapped second. Little Whiskey screamed her lungs out and crested the top on her first go. Without the heavy burden of my kit, my little bike made it look easy.

I went up and down a few more times; some I didn't quite make, and the windswept sand would suck my back wheel back in. Luckily there were plenty of other travellers to help me get her up.

On top of the dune was a large flat area where others had come to watch the sunset. It was an incredible evening to be in the desert. Standing on top of that dune, the sun's rays warming my face, I gazed around me in awe. The sky was a kaleidoscope of colour: the sun, a giant burning ball low on the horizon, while wispy strands of cirrus clouds filled the sky like a crimson head of hair flung back in the breeze. The sand at my feet had a deep glow, as if they were the coals of a dying fire. From the base of the sand dune stretched a giant clay pan, its sparse vegetation casting long dark shadows across the rugged terrain. It was breathtaking.

I knew on the following morning I would cross that pan and spend the next two to three weeks chasing the setting sun into the vast deserts of the west. This was the true beginning of my odyssey but I felt at ease, undaunted. The desert has a certain energy about it; it's a magical place. I could feel its energy as I sat and watched the clouds move through the sky, though I didn't know how I would ever explain it to people.

I eventually made camp on the clay pan and woke early the next day to ride up to the second dune and watch the sun rise up over Big Red from the east. With the weight of my saddlebags, my bike only got half way up before I had to stop, unpack, and haul my gear the rest of the way up. I got the last of my gear to the top as the sun was rising, and started the tea brewing while I got my breath back. It was an impressive sight. I looked out across the endless dunes in front of me to the west. I knew I would need to dig deep today. There was going to be a lot of pushing up the dunes, unloading and reloading my gear. My bike was loaded for forty days, so that was no small task.

I was so hyper-focused on getting the job done that I forgot to eat that whole first day. By the time the sun was three fingers off the horizon, I was spent. I found a flat piece of bush to make camp.

The nights were cold in the Simpson. I woke with ice on my tent each morning, and in the mornings my sodden boots (wet from a river crossing) made my feet numb for the first hour or so. I met other people along the way and was grateful for their support. I even met another group of motorbike riders with a support vehicle. These guys invited me to camp with them, but I kept pushing on. I opted to camp alone and maintain my focus. I had a job to do, and drinking beers around the campfire would have been a distraction.

On the morning of the third day I was trying to play catch-up with my past energy. My unconditioned body was screaming at me to stop. Around mid-morning, I passed a lone four-by-four and asked them for some snacks; I had eaten all mine and had only ready-to-eat meals left. They gave me two raw eggs that I cracked straight into my mouth. The energy I felt was immediately noticeable; I have a newfound respect for eggs and their nutritional value.

That afternoon, the track twisted and turned. The dunes got bigger and bigger, separated by wide, open clay pans of hard-baked earth and coarse undergrowth. I'd look forever forward, picking my lines across the rugged ground and undulating landscape while the dunes rose up at me like waves in a huge ocean swell, as if to challenge me further, as if daring me to keep going. I thought about the bike riders I'd met and their empty bike rack. It would have been easy to catch them, store my bike, and get a ride out. *No, Brundin, this is what you signed up for! Let's keep going.*

The dunes were relentless. I decided to unsling my heavy backpack and strap it to the rear of my bike. My shoulders thanked me, but the very next dune laughed at me, sucking my back wheel in deep past the axle. I spent the next hour digging it out and walking all my gear up the mountain of sand. Lesson learnt. My boots were full of sand, my hands rubbed raw from gripping the handlebars and hanging off the back[4]. The sweat was pouring off me but at least the flies were friendly. I finally pulled into Dalhousie Springs after the sun had set.

It had taken me three full days to cross the Simpson. The sheer physicality of the journey had nearly broken me at times. I was exhausted, but totally elated. I just couldn't believe I had done it! It was one of the most epic things I had ever achieved.

Soaking in those thermal pools was heaven; they were like God's gift to all those who successfully survive the desert crossing. I rode to Oodnadatta the next day and gave myself the treat of three T-bone steaks for dinner before riding on to Coober Pedy for the next leg of the expedition.

From Coober Pedy, the next challenge was the Great Victorian Desert, the largest desert in Australia. I knew from my research that this would be the most isolated leg of the whole journey, and would present a whole different set of monsters to overcome.

There was no fuel or water resupply for nearly 800 km from my current position, and nearly 1800 km to my destination in the far west. To prepare for this, I took twenty-one litres of water and forty-six litres of fuel, and I allowed four days to get to the next checkpoint. My ten-day resupply of food weighed just over six kilograms, and my riding kit and utility belt weighed about twenty kilograms dry. I normally stood on tippy-toe when I sat on my bike, but now my

---

4   Leaning back into the bike to keep your balance and your weight off the front end when going over sandy terrain.

heels were firmly on the ground. The bike was Moby Dick and I was Captain Ahab. Only now I hoped that this particular whale didn't take my leg.

But I couldn't shake an uneasy feeling. I called my sister Leah and she pepped me up. I stopped a priest in the street and recited the 'Our Father' together. That was crazy, because I'm not even religious. In the end, I knew I was just stalling; I had to suck it up and head out into the desert.

On the first day, I saw only one car travelling east. I also saw the tyre marks of an adventure rider I knew who'd planned a similar ride and had been along the same track thirteen days previously. We had supported one another in our prep. His tracks in the sand gave me a feeling of security that someone had been through before me; I didn't feel quite so alone. However, I tried not to think about the fact that Slip didn't make it through and spent a few very long and painful days in the bush waiting for rescue.

On the second day, the sand kept getting deeper, the track tighter. During the afternoon, I rode across a long stretch of badly burnt land. I had a really unsettled feeling as I rode over the remains of the desolate bush. It was weird: the fire had gone through years ago but nothing had returned to life. As I rode, I felt that the charred bodies of the dead trees were staring right through me, offended by my presence, their clawed branches pointing at me to move on. It was an intense feeling. I kept my head down and my throttle open through that stretch. At one point I rode past an old abandoned airfield. The tattered remains of an old windsock hung limply against its mast. Forty-four-gallon fuel drums lay in a rusted heap, riddled with bullet holes. The airfield had serviced the atomic testing area back in the fifties. A feeling of sadness and deep loss pervaded the whole region.

On the third day I woke with stiff legs: my body was in shock from the amount of punishment I was dishing out. I stood up slowly, mentally preparing myself for another day of sand. I still couldn't shake that unsettled feeling so I checked and rechecked my kit. It wasn't long before the problems started to pop up.

Around mid-morning, I crested a sand dune and bounced my bike like a pinball off a tree. Somehow, I managed to keep the bike upright and power out of the sand. But when I pulled up, I had burst one of my water bottles. One and a half litres equates to about six hours of life out there. Not long after that, I lost the nipple on my bladder and with it another twelve hours of life flowed out of my backpack. Shit! I did a quick mental sitrep (Situation Report).

I was nearly 500 km from the nearest town. I had only seen two sets of cars in nearly three days, and my only companions were Slip's wheel marks in the sand. At the current rate, I had nearly two days of travel to get to my next resupply, and less than a day of good water left. The situation wasn't horrible, but I knew I had to make up some ground or spend a very thirsty day on the bike. I bottled my urine from then on, and even made a video of me making a cocktail of urine, water, Berocca and hydrolyte, and swilling it down like a pint of beer.

Then the sandstorm came blowing in. Gusts of wind started pushing me across the track; they blew the wheel ruts clean. As I stopped to fix yet another water leak, I watched my own tracks blow away. Then suddenly Slip's tracks, which I'd become quite attached to, also disappeared. Suddenly I felt very alone, vulnerable and afraid.

All right, Brundin, this is it. We are in it now. Deep breath. Breathe. You'll be fine, mate. Stay upright, stay alive, keep winning – you got that! Keep living, keep winning!

In the desert, the difference between winning and losing was living and dying. Every day I made it through, I was winning.

I rode close to 350 km that day. I was completely immersed in the bush around me. I don't remember the exact moment it happened but a clear vision came into my mind that stuck with me throughout that day as my poor little bike screamed through the gears and over the dunes like it was riding for its life.

I pulled into the Ilkurlka Roadhouse as the last light was leaving the sky. The resident caretaker, Rob, took one look at me and offered me the spare bed in the caretaker's cabin. I was so grateful. The thought of setting up my camp was enough to make me want to cry at that moment.

The first thing I did was to call home to let Jenny know I was safe. They hadn't heard from me for a few days. The desert had been incredibly challenging emotionally and, as I spoke to Jenny, I felt incredible relief wash over me.

"I made it. I'm alive. Something happened out there, Jen. I'm going to tell you something that you need to hold me accountable to. One day, I am going to have little brown babies running around my feet. And I am going to build a big long wooden table that I'm going to fill with my family and all the people I love." This vision was so clear to me. It was crystal clear.

I spent the next two days riding through some of the most corrugated parts of the entire expedition; they made it by far the most treacherous and isolated leg. The evidence of flooding rains was clear everywhere as cavernous trenches of eroded clay appeared out of nowhere. Some of these washouts were big enough to swallow a truck. At one point, I was riding in an eroded section of track where the walls of the washout were over a metre high either side of my bike. It was like riding into a canyon that got deeper and deeper. The walls got tighter and tighter until there was nowhere to get out further ahead and I had to stop and retreat. It took quite a bit of manoeuvring to back out.

Unlike the Simpson, or the Great Vic Desert, the Gibson proved to be extremely rocky and shaley terrain to ride over; I was forever dodging huge boulders and rocky outcrops. One afternoon, late in the day, the land suddenly fell away into a giant ravine. Below me stretched a huge savannah of coarse bushland. It went on forever and reminded me of Africa's Rift Valley.

I decided to take a break, refuel my bike, and grab a bite to eat. Sitting on the ledge of a huge rock, my feet dangling in the air below, I watched the sun fall lower in the sky. It was so peaceful. There wasn't another person as far as the eye could see; the isolation was complete. It was beautiful. I let my mind wander to thoughts of days gone by, to the life I had left behind. Then I broke discipline and let myself make a call on my Sat phone. The dial tone rang out and went to message bank. I licked my cracked lips as I spoke; my voice was coarse from the dry, the dust, and the lack of use.

"Hi, Scarlett, it's me, Benji. I'm somewhere in the desert at the moment. A few things have happened in my life since we last spoke. I just wanted to let you know I'm okay, that I am so grateful for the life we had together and all we shared. Thank you, Scarlett; you are an incredible person. I hope you're happy now and that life is going well. Anyway, I am doing something kind of special at the moment and just wanted you to know that. Hope you hear about it. Keep your fingers crossed for me. Love, Benji."

That night, I shed a tear for all that had been. It wasn't for sorrow or sadness – those tears had fallen long ago; it felt like it was for acceptance: my time of mourning was passing, and I could look back fondly on all we once had, as opposed to all that could have been.

Scarlett eventually remarried. Although we kept in brief contact for a while, we no longer had a reason to stay in each other's lives. She went on to get promotion after promotion in her field, and moved with her new partner into the suburbs somewhere. He is a decent man, well educated and white-collared. I don't know if they have any kids. I am just really glad that she found happiness once again. She spent the better part of our eight years together trying to save me from my past. In the end, even she realized that only I could do that.

When I look back on the time we spent together, I think of endless fits of laughter, long sleep-ins, and walks in the park with Bruce.

Scarlett came into my life at a time when I felt totally void of any real love for people. I had spent the better part of my childhood moving around the country, and as a result, never felt like I belonged anywhere. She showed me what it really meant to love a person, and for a while she really did save me; for a time I was certain that I had found my place of belonging in life. She showed me that I was worthy of love, and for that, I will always be grateful.

I still sometimes think of her and of the memories we shared. But those moments become fewer and fewer as times goes by. She will always hold a special place in my heart. I wish her all the best.

On the morning of my fourteenth day in the deserts I was close to pulling into the Warburton Roadhouse and the halfway point – halfway of nearly 8000 kms! I was exhausted. My body was broken and I just wanted to go home. Every kilometre west from here was another torturous kilometre away from Victoria. I was at a mental fork in the road.

I wrote the following sitrep:

23 July, morning, feeling sore.

5 days on pegs

3 days no cars

Muscles sore

Back and traps sore from heavy pack – 15 kg

Feet, palms blistered

Hands numb, no feeling in my right three fingers

Hard work

Freezing, shivered all night

Feel my clothes getting bigger, losing weight

No human contact

Bike has been tortured – how can it keep going?

Only halfway

I chose this life. I wanted this journey, this challenge. My friends and family told me I was crazy, that it couldn't be done. Who do I think I am? Pure insanity, no one has ever done it! Yet I spent the money, I bought the equipment and supplies, I trained and I've persevered with it. Love it or hate it, it's up to me. I can go home any time. Win or lose, live or die, it's all on me. Everything depends on how I perceive it. Get up, Brundin. Get up and own this life!

This was the moment I had been training my mind and body for ever since hiking through the night at Wilsons Prom. I had been building on my reserves of resilience since deciding to go on that night, and then again on the beaches of Robe, at Fitzgerald River, Kakadu, flipping my bike on the Creb Track… All those crazy adventures had brought me here, to this moment.

There comes a time, a moment in every adventure, whether it be a sporting game, an expedition or a business venture, when things get hard, stressful and overwhelming. This is the defining moment, the moment where you can turn back and give up, or push on into the unknown and extend your realm of possibility. Most people take the easy option, but if you really want to push yourself and see what is possible, then this is it.

Defining moments like these will separate you from the rest of the pack. My question to you is simply this: *When your moment comes, what choice will you make?*

For me, that morning was a real moment out there. The cumulative exhaustion had pushed me right to the edge; I just wanted to give up, to stop, but I chose to push on. I didn't realize it at the time, but after owning those decisions and accepting the pain as part of the journey, things would start to get easier.

In the seven days since leaving Coober Pedy, I had seen only five cars, all going east. When I finally rode into Carnegie station, I was grateful for a real shower, a hot meal and some human contact. It had been a mental battle more than a physical one to get that far, and it had been everything I had hoped it would be. Battered but not beaten, I was totally elated. I took the next day off and went out with the cowboys to muster some cattle for the day. It was a great experience, one I was grateful for. Helping them paid for my meals and lodging for another night, and then I was onto the final leg of this odyssey – Wiluna and the Canning Stock Route.

The Canning Stock Route (CSR) was originally built in 1908 by a man named Alfred Canning to allow cattle men to drove their cattle from the Kimberley in the north of the state to the town of Wiluna further south. To water the cattle and horses that used the route, fifty-one wells had been bored along the route. A lot of these are now in ruins but some have been restored to provide drinkable water. The CSR is widely considered to be one of great four-wheel drive adventures in the world. The track is unmaintained, however, and burnt-out shells of once expensive four-wheel drives are a common sight. The CSR crosses three deserts. It stretches over 1850 km and is the longest historic stock route in the world. There are no towns or medical services along the route. It is one of the most remote tracks in Australia.

I spent a day in Wiluna, resting up and servicing my bike. I met a dozen or so travellers who had just finished the CSR north to south, so I sat around their campfire and interrogated them about the track and what I could expect.

"The track is in its worst condition ever," they told me. "A single motorbike just won't get through. It's bloody hard work, even in the four-bys. The dunes are massive!"

They were scoffing at me. I let them have their say, took what they said on board, and thanked them all. I had heard it all before. But there was something different now. I didn't realize it at the time, but the fear coiling around in my stomach that I had become so accustomed to wasn't there anymore. I had beaten the monster. And in doing so, I had expanded my horizon of possibility. I was learning a lot about myself and about the nature of fear.

After all I had come across, I knew I could do it. I knew that I *would* do it. I had just 2000 km left of the wildest, most remote desert track in the country to traverse, and it wasn't scaring me at all.

I went into the CSR with excitement and open-mindedness in my heart; I felt very different to when I was beginning the other legs of the journey. Because of this, the incredible nature of people really started to shine through, and I experienced many 'miracles'.

On the morning of the first day, I met Will and Lorraine; they were kind people and I could sense their concern for me when I left them. Later on they would tell me they prayed for me every night they made camp. I would cross paths with them again and again throughout this journey. The first day was also when the crazy stuff started to happen. I hate wearing my goggles when I ride and prefer my sunglasses so the wind can cool my face while I'm riding. But I'd lost my sunnies; I just couldn't find them anywhere. Frustrated, I had resigned myself to the fact that I would have to wear my goggles. Not more than a few kilometres down the track, a branch speared into my lenses like a javelin, pulling my face back and my bike into the bush. Had I been wearing my sunnies, I would have lost an eye at least.

I was riding across the CSR with a fully loaded bike; it was similar to the load I had taken into the Great Victoria Desert, only now the track had so many twists and turns it was incredibly hard going just keeping the bike upright. I found myself pushing the bike up sand dunes once again. By the end of the second day, I had managed under 400 km. I was exhausted as I set camp at Well 13. My nutrition starting out from Wiluna hadn't been the best and I felt I had been playing catch-up all over again. I had planned to gorge on delicious pub food when I got to Wiluna, only to find there was no pub and the local store didn't have much on offer, so it had been deep fried fish and chips for dinner. While I got a fire going, I questioned my motives for continuing. I had proven everything I needed to in the first twenty days. What was the point of going on?

Then a set of headlights came into view and soon I was meeting Cheryl and Ray. For some reason, they had decided to keep driving into the night where normally they would have set camp around 4 p.m. Cheryl took one look at me and proceeded to mother me like a child. She cooked me a dinner of steamed veggies and barbecue chicken, and Ray set the shower up and let me have a wash. Their kindness reinspired me: a warm shower and a hot meal made a mountain of difference to my headspace. In the morning, Cheryl wouldn't let me carry on without cooking bacon and eggs first and giving me a pre-cooked meal for the road.

The track continued forever north. I met a tour group of pensioners at a popular campground and they all peppered me with questions about my journey. Every time I met a group of cars, the look I got was always the same. People just could not believe that I was out there all alone. They would offer food and water, they would take photos with their kids, they would shake my hand and squeeze it with admiration. Their support inspired me to keep going.

By the time I was 850 km into the track, I realized that what I was doing was a bit special. My whole life I had wanted to prove I was capable of doing the impossible, and now I was actually doing it. The self-doubt that had hung like a cloud over me was finally beginning to lift. One night, I made a camera diary where I spoke about not being able to go back to my old life. After all that I had overcome and achieved out here, I knew that I had more to give the world than what I had been giving it. I had been living life on the fence. It was time to stop being a passenger, and instead, to get into the game of life and play full on. I vowed that I would no longer be just another puppet on a string.

The next day I rode into an Aboriginal community to pick up my resupply and refuel. That led to a meeting with the school principal, which led to me doing a talk with the kids about my adventure, which led to an invitation to go into the bush with them for a day. It was a very rare opportunity to spend time with the local kids, and made me realize once again what I really loved doing.

From my resupply point, I continued north into the tropics. From then on, the occupants of every car I ran into wanted to get a photo and chat. They'd all heard of some guy on a motorbike attempting to set a new world record. One time I was sitting under a tree eating my lunch when a tour group of over fifteen cars crested the dunes in front of me. People stopped to shake my hand and get the photos. What can I say? It made me feel pretty special inside.

The riding itself didn't get any easier. The track could change dramatically from deep sand to sharp rocky outcrops. There was never a time I felt I could relax, and there were some real 'oh shit' moments. I just don't know how I survived.

Sometimes the track was so tight that four-by-fours had to push the dead trees over in the path. I can't tell you how many times I turned a corner, only to see the branches of a dead tree pointing straight at me like the spears from Mel Gibson's movie *Braveheart*. I would try to avoid them but I lost count of how many of those spears I pulled out of my saddlebags. I actually got used to bouncing off the trees and termite mounds. I would laugh nervously every time I did, but somehow, I stayed upright. I had to start asking cars for spare cable ties because every seam on my saddlebags had burst. And the rocks! Giant reefs of iron and stone would just appear out of the sand. I would wince as I bounced over them, certain that my ride was now over and both my tyres would surely be blown. When they weren't, I laughed to myself and carried on.

I met other travellers who had been harassed by dingoes and wild dogs in every camp they'd set. I had also seen the dogs around. One night I saw a few, snouts to the ground, sniffing out prey on the sand dunes across from me. In the morning there were hundreds of mouse tracks around my camp, but no dingo tracks. Despite being such an easy target out there, I never once had my gear taken or my camp ransacked. They left me alone, which I thought was odd.

One day I passed a Landcruiser and the couple in it were kind enough to give me some oranges to eat. Later in the day, I decided to have lunch in the shade of some desert oaks. I savoured the process of carefully cutting the oranges into quarters. As I placed them down, away from the sand, I realized it had been over three weeks since my last piece of fruit. My mouth was watering as I devoured them. I put one in my tank bag and looked forward to it all the next morning, in anticipation of a delicious lunch once again.

On the morning of my twenty-eighth day in the desert, I felt there was something amiss on my bike. I pulled into Well 41 to have a quick bath and repack my kit. There I met a convoy of travellers who also loved motorbikes. I got talking with a few, which distracted me from going over my bike properly as I would normally do. I was going to leave once my shirt had dried but decided to stop and say hi to the owners of a big Unimog.

Steve, a mechanic by trade, had been repairing a punctured tyre. He took one look at my bike and simply said, "You're not going to get very far without that." He pointed down to where a nut was missing that held my subframe and engine together. Would you believe it, he even had the right-sized nut in his toolbox to keep me going? What were the odds of losing your nut out here, only to pull into a camp and find a replacement? I was dancing and hugging both Steve and Carol. These guys saved my life! After that, I was convinced that 'someone' was looking out for me.

I rode all day with that convoy, and really enjoyed getting to meet and know them all. They were a great bunch. That night I was mothered by Carol, with fish fillets, roast potatoes and coleslaw for dinner, followed by scones and blueberry damper for dessert. I was spoilt rotten.

The next day, I woke feeling fresh as a daisy. I had less than 350 km left and wanted to get it done. My time in camp with the Unimoggers was the perfect way to sign off on the CSR.

"Thanks again, guys, for everything. Really, I mean that."

"Just pay it forward, mate, just pay it forward." Steve's words struck a chord with me. I decided to make sure that I would.

That last day on the Canning I tore through the bush with all the confidence of a man on a mission. I passed Will and Lorraine from Well 1 again. It was good to see them, the first people I'd met and now almost the last. It was also good to thank them for their support and let them know how great it was to see their car coming over the dunes this last ten days. It was my turn to say, "God bless you both."

I tore across the dunes all day. It was reckless, dangerous. I nearly had a head-on with a jeep at one point.

I stopped in at Well 49 to have a quick wash and eat. For people going south, it's their first day. They are full of excitement and nervous energy. One older guy stopped to chat. He'd got lost at the turn-off to Well 49 and wished he had a better map. He asked my thoughts on taking a GPS. His white beard was freshly clipped and well groomed, his crisp safari shirt freshly ironed. His little old wife was taking selfies at the well as we spoke. I could see in his eyes what he was thinking – I looked like I had just ridden out of hell. I was short with him as I scrubbed my face and poured water straight down my jacket front. I didn't want to chat to people too long.

"How far you going, mate?"

"All the way, young man."

"Best to wait for another convoy. You just won't make it alone. You're not prepared, you have no gear. The track will have you, mate. I gotta go. Good luck."

"Can we get a photo?"

"Take it as I'm leaving. See ya."

I continued to tear through the bush but, just before I got to Well 51, my front tyre washed out on an off-camber stretch of track. I can remember the world moving in slow motion as I bounced across the corrugations on my side and watched my bike sliding across the dust doing 360s. That one hurt and could have been bad. But I picked myself up, dusted myself off, and kept going. That night I couldn't turn in my sleep; my hip and backside were tender from the slide.

The next day, I made it up onto the rim of the Wolf Creek Crater. I had envisioned myself standing there a thousand times. Now I had made it. I had successfully crossed every desert in Australia. I only had to cross the Tanami Desert (via another long corrugated road) to finish this trip off.

I ate some lunch up there, met some fellow travellers, and made a video. I was feeling pretty happy with myself, but it hadn't quite hit me that it was nearly all over. I camped in the Tanami Desert that night and spoilt myself with calls on the sat phone to the people I loved. They just couldn't believe it. I could hear it in their voices. *I couldn't believe it!*

The next morning, I crossed the state border. It was a fitting place to sign off as a marker point should anyone else ever want to attempt to break my record.

"That's it, Benji, ten deserts, finished, done. The crowd goes wild!" and I panned my camera around to show the vast nothingness around me.

I had been in the deserts for thirty days – nearly forty since leaving Melbourne. It had been twenty months and ten days since I had first ridden a motorbike. I was still technically on my Learners!

I continued my ride back towards Alice Springs. I could relax, I thought, and put my earphones in to listen to some music as I rode – the first time on the whole trip. No sooner had I done that, my back tyre finally gave up and had a pretty bad blowout. I laughed. Nothing could bring me down at that moment.

A four-wheel drive stopped to help me change it. The repair didn't last, and I ended up riding another 30 to 40 km on my blown rear into a remote mining camp deep in the heart of the Tanami Desert. The girl at the security gate saw me approaching: my back end was wagging up the road like the tail of a dog. I hadn't shaved or changed my dusted clothes in over a month. My boots were held together with electrical tape; the clips torn off from countless branches brushing past them. My feet were blistered, my eyes bloodshot, I had lost close to ten kilograms in the last thirty days and my face was gaunt and haggard. I looked like I had ridden straight out of a Mad Max movie.

My battle-weary bike was in no better condition. There were over a hundred cable ties holding my saddlebags together. The bark busters[5] were bent, broken and out of shape; the white plastics were stained red from the dust of Australia; and my indicator was swinging from its perch like a tea bag.

The security girl had a particular look on her face, one I had become accustomed to seeing this past month.

I met her stare with a big cheesy grin. She looked confused as my smile didn't match the dirty, ragged sight she was presented with.

"What the hell are you doing out here, mate? Where the hell have you been?"

"I just came out of the desert."

---

5   Plastic covers on the handlebars that protect your knuckles from branches and scrub as you ride.

"Jesus, you're bloody game. Why are you so happy?"

"I just set a new Guinness World Record!" And my smile grew wider again.

The Canning Stock Route:
https://www.youtube.com/watch?v=rEdmdeOM8ok

Standing on the top of Big Red, Simpson Desert, July 2019

Sunset in the desert

Bogged in deep sand. The Simpson Desert.

Leaving Coober Pedy with my hatchet tied to my saddle bag to help support the weight.

The cowboys of Carnegie Station

Cresting a dune in the Great Sandy Desert

Steve and Carol's Unimog CSR

The Unimog bogged on a dune

Well 41, Canning Stock Route, 6 August 2019

Changing flats in the desert, still smiling

Signing off after crossing the ten. Tanami Desert, August 8, 2019

Guinness World Record® Certificate: The fastest time to cross all ten Australian deserts on motorbike is 29 days 19 hours and 38 minutes and was achieved by Benjamen Brundin (Australia) in the Tanami Desert, Australia, on 8 August 2019

Be Brave
KEEP LIVING, KEEP WINNING.

Benji Brundin

My time in the deserts had a profound effect on me but I only appreciated how profound when I got back to Melbourne.

Everything in me had changed but nothing had changed at home. I immediately felt the dull pull of society nagging at me to live and be a certain way. I resisted. I kept living in my van in the back streets of suburbia while I tried to transition back into normality – without really wanting to. People looked at me like I was a bum. I felt like a misfit.

I crashed pretty hard and struggled to understand the next step for me. Part of me wanted to head straight back out into the wilderness, part of me wanted to reconnect with old friends and the things I used to love to do. But old friends had families now – their purpose was clear; mine was not. Another part of me wanted to find a way of giving everything I'd learnt to society.

Writing this book helped me. It brought me back to the beginning of the journey, reminding me of the state I'd been in when I left and of everything I'd learnt along the way, and it gave me a means of sharing those insights with people who are struggling as I had struggled.

Mental health issues in our communities are more common than they have ever been. Did you know that suicide is the leading cause of death in Australians aged fifteen to forty-four years? Men are twice as likely to take their lives as women, and these figures are higher again in indigenous and gay communities. With all the stress and pressure of social media adding to the mix, it's no wonder these figures are so staggering. Despite more and more acceptance of mental illness, people who experience signs and symptoms of depression and anxiety rarely seek medical help because of the stigma that is still attached to it. This mentality has to change if things are ever going to get better. Mental health issues do not discriminate: everyone battles something.

Too many of the people I love have lost their lives to suicide. If I can use the success of this ride for anything it will be to bring awareness to the fact that dark experiences hold the key to our greatest growth. To win, you need courage, the courage to be authentically you and not let fear dictate the terms of your life. You need to stand firm in the face of adversity and state boldly:

I will not stand by and be told how to live.

I will not be dictated to.

I am worthy *just because I am me.*

I will not be pulled down and thrown into a corner.

I have the power to be incredible, to create any life I choose.

I am enough.

I am worthy.

I am brave.

I am beautiful.

I am completely me.

Be brave, stand firm, and you will win.

Acknowledgements

The first person I would like to thank is Shane (Whitey) Kennedy. It was during my darkest struggles that this man stood up and opened his home to me. Friendships are tried and tested on the battlefields of life, and this man sat in the trenches with me through the longest nights. Thank you, Whiteman. A true gentleman.

To the Bininj People of Kakadu and the incredible people I got to share my adventures with in that part of the world: Thank you for opening your beautiful lands to me and showing me one of the most incredible places on earth.

To Victor 'The Wizard': Thank you for always working your magic and constantly showing me that nothing is impossible.

To Jenny: Thank you for always picking up the phone, no matter what time of day or night, and always having the time to share a hot cup of tea.

To my incredible family, whether your hair is red, brown, blonde, black or blue – you all know who you are: I am so grateful to have all of you in my life. Thank you for just being you, and for all your support during my crazy adventures.

To Brandon and the team at Bobby Dunne's Boxing Gym. You guys all came into my life at just the right time and taught me how to focus my energy constructively. This came in handy once or twice in the wild places. Cheers, gents.

To Kylie Bartlett, my mentor: Thank you for seeing potential in me and guiding me through the whole publishing process. Your knowledge and insights have been priceless.

To my editor, Liliane Grace: Thank you, thank you, thank you! You proved time and again that your attention to detail is impeccable! You took the rambling words of an emotional roof tiler and made them into something respectable. I am forever indebted to you.

To the team behind the success of the Ten Desert Odyssey; Stel, Darren, Bec, Sally, Shahn, Mel, Ryan, and all my sponsors. Thank you for all your belief in me and my crazy ambitions. I could never have done it without you.

To David Alenson from Alenson Design: Thank you for all your hard work behind the scenes on logos, website content and cover designs, and for countless hours of conversations about maps and colours, etc etc. Thanks for all your patience, mate. You're a legend.

To Jeremy at Shevek Creative: Thank you for all your work behind the scenes with typesetting, emails, and all my other requests that are technically beyond me.

To Jarrod, thank you for being such a good brother to me, not just in recent years, but since forever. Your selfless character has always seen you putting yourself second. That will never be lost on me. In moments of darkness, you have always been the lighthouse I have sought. Thank you, Jarrod. From the bottom of my heart, thank you.

And to my incredible mother: Although you left us almost 20 years ago, I feel you with me still. On the floodplains of Kakadu or in the sands of the Simpson, you have been with me every step of the way. Guiding my heart in the right direction. Working hard to keep me upright. My beautiful mother. Thank you for your fighting spirit, your love, your life. I feel you with me now and always.

And finally, for you, the reader: Thank you for picking up my book. I hope it has in some way inspired you to get out there and start fighting for all the things you want in your life.

FOR FULL PHOTO GALLERY AND MUCH MORE VISIT:
WWW.DARING2VENTURE.COM.AU

FOR ALL EVENT
AND PUBLIC SPEAKING
ENQUIRIES PLEASE EMAIL:
BENJI@DARING2VENTURE.COM.AU

DARING2VENTURE

DARING2VENTURE

DARING 2VENTURE

STAY TUNED FOR
THE NEXT BIG
ADVENTURE!

Benjamen Augusto Roca Brundin (b. 12 June 1983) is the middle child of a Filipino mother and a Swedish immigrant father. Born in the Pilbara region of Western Australia, he spent his childhood exploring the vast desert that stretched for miles at the rear of his home.

His mother, a proud woman, kicked his father out when Benji was five, stating that she could simply do a better job without him. It was his mother who encouraged Benji to journal his thoughts and adventures from a young age.

In 1995 she bought a small zoo with her then partner, and Benji and his two siblings moved with them across the country to Victoria. It was here that Benji met the people who would one day become the guiding lights of his developmental years.

At age 19, after finishing a roofing apprenticeship and feeling a deep desire for an adventurous life, he embarked on a road trip around Australia. Just months into this trip, his mother died suddenly of cancer; Benji chose to curtail his travels to protect his younger brother from a life in the foster care system. Benji and his brother Nonoy are still close and are proud of their mother and their Filipino heritage.

So far, Benji has been a boxer, a sailor, a husband and a public servant. He has written two books and is a mentor to young people. Constantly looking for ways to challenge himself, he set a new Guinness world record in 2019 when he became the first person to cross all ten Australian deserts, solo and unsupported, on a motorbike.

Lightning Source UK Ltd.
Milton Keynes UK
UKHW022048140421
381996UK00009B/1993